The Complete Mediterranean Diet Cookbook for Beginners

1500 Days of Healthy & Tasty Recipes for Embracing the Mediterranean Lifestyle | 90-Day Customized Meal Plan Included | Premium Color Pictures

Clara Marelli

Copyright © 2022

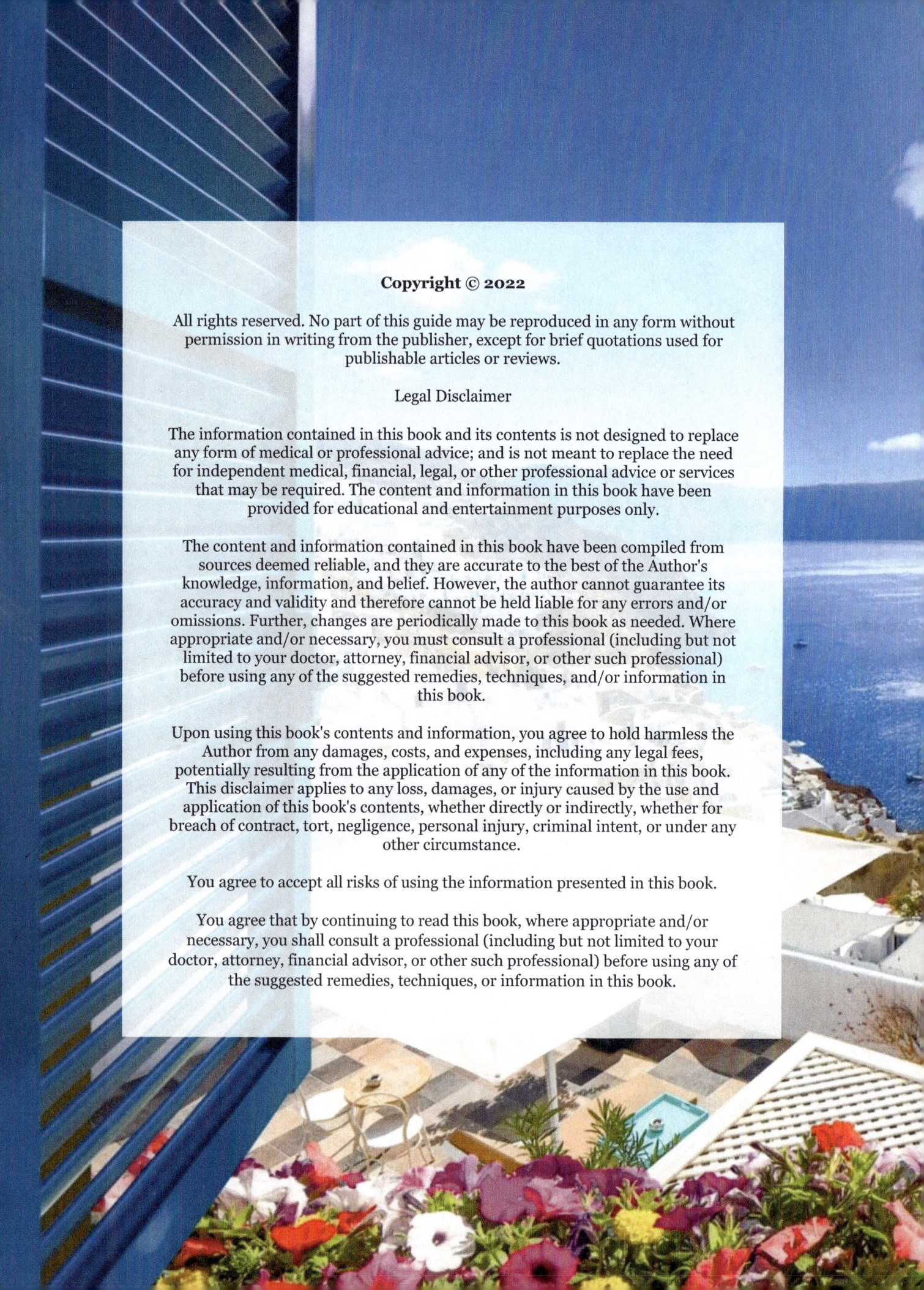

All rights reserved. No part of this guide may be reproduced in any form without permission in writing from the publisher, except for brief quotations used for publishable articles or reviews.

Legal Disclaimer

The information contained in this book and its contents is not designed to replace any form of medical or professional advice; and is not meant to replace the need for independent medical, financial, legal, or other professional advice or services that may be required. The content and information in this book have been provided for educational and entertainment purposes only.

The content and information contained in this book have been compiled from sources deemed reliable, and they are accurate to the best of the Author's knowledge, information, and belief. However, the author cannot guarantee its accuracy and validity and therefore cannot be held liable for any errors and/or omissions. Further, changes are periodically made to this book as needed. Where appropriate and/or necessary, you must consult a professional (including but not limited to your doctor, attorney, financial advisor, or other such professional) before using any of the suggested remedies, techniques, and/or information in this book.

Upon using this book's contents and information, you agree to hold harmless the Author from any damages, costs, and expenses, including any legal fees, potentially resulting from the application of any of the information in this book. This disclaimer applies to any loss, damages, or injury caused by the use and application of this book's contents, whether directly or indirectly, whether for breach of contract, tort, negligence, personal injury, criminal intent, or under any other circumstance.

You agree to accept all risks of using the information presented in this book.

You agree that by continuing to read this book, where appropriate and/or necessary, you shall consult a professional (including but not limited to your doctor, attorney, financial advisor, or other such professional) before using any of the suggested remedies, techniques, or information in this book.

TABLE OF CONTENTS

Introduction 1
- Mediterranean Food Culture Through History ... 1
- What is the Mediterranean Diet? 2
- Key Habits to Feel Healthier 2
  - Be More Active 2
  - Dine With Others 3
  - Manage Your Stress 3
  - Live Simply 3
  - Work Out..................... 4
- Why is This Diet Famous and its Potential Benefits . 4
  - Potential Benefits........... 5
  - Promotes Heart Health..5
  - Maintain Healthy Blood Sugar Levels 5
  - Protect Brain Function ..5
- What to Eat and What to Limit 5
  - Foods to Eat 5
  - Foods to Limit 6
  - What About Beverages? 6
  - Snack Options 6
- Measurement Conversion Table 6
  - Volumes 6
  - Temperature 7
  - Weight 7

Chapter 1: Breakfast Recipes 8
- Yogurt with Caramelized Figs................................. 9
- Yogurt Oatmeal................. 9
- Avocado & Eggs Toast 9
- Yogurt Waffles 10
- Ricotta Pancakes.............. 10
- Mixed Veggie Muffins...... 10
- Multi-Grain Bread 11
- Potato Omelet 11
- Shakshuka....................... 12
- Ham Quiche 12

Chapter 2: Meze, Antipasti & Appetizer Recipes 13
- Cucumber & Walnut Platter 13
- Tahini Potato Platter 13
- Tabbouleh Platter 14
- Antipasti Layered Dip...... 14
- Deli Meat Antipasti........... 15
- Deli Meat & Veggie Antipasti........................ 15
- Toasted Ravioli 15
- Fried Mozzarella 16
- Stuffed Mushrooms 16
- Tuna Croquettes 17

Chapter 3: Salads & Soups Recipes 18
- Chicken Salad 18
- Steak Salad....................... 18
- Chickpeas Salad 19
- Watermelon Salad 19
- Greens & Carrot Salad 20
- Chicken Soup 20
- Meatballs Soup 21
- Lamb Soup 21
- Quinoa & Lentil Soup 22
- Tomato Soup.................... 22

Chapter 4: Vegetarian Mains Recipes 23
- Cheesy Spinach Bake 23
- Eggplant Parmesan......... 23
- Eggplant Lasagna............ 24
- Summer Squash Gratin .. 24
- Potato Gratin 25
- Mushroom Galette 25
- Cabbage Casserole 26
- Mushroom Bourguignon 26
- Zoodles with Mushroom Sauce 27
- Ratatouille....................... 27
- Squash & Fruit Bake 28
- Veggie Coq Au Vin 28
- Baked Veggie Stew 29
- Veggie-Stuffed Cabbage Rolls 29
- Gnocchi with Tomato & Wine Sauce...................... 30

Chapter 5: Fish & Seafood Recipes 31
- Salmon with Capers 31
- Salmon with Avocado Sauce 31
- Salmon in Creamy Sauce 32
- Tilapia Piccata................. 32
- Tilapia with Raisins 33
- Halibut Parcel 33
- Cod with Tomatoes 34
- Tuna with Olives 34
- Tuna in Wine Sauce 35
- Garlicky Prawns 35
- Shrimp Casserole 35
- Mussels in Wine Sauce ... 36

Octopus in Tomato Sauce 36
Seafood Bake 37
Seafood Stew 37

Chapter 6: Poultry & Meat Recipes 38
Chicken Pita Pockets 38
Bruschetta Chicken 39
Braised Chicken Thighs .. 39
Spiced Chicken Stew 40
Turkey Burgers 40
Stuffed Leg of Lamb 41
Wine Infused Lamb Shanks 41
Pistachio-Topped Lamb Chops 42
Lamb Koftas 42
Steak with Yogurt Sauce .. 43
Stuffed Steak 43
Tomato Braised Beef 44
Pork Chops with Mushroom Sauce 44
Sausage with Bell Peppers 45
Wild Boar Stew 45

Chapter 7: Rice & Grains Recipes 46
Rice with Pork 46
Rice with Beans 46
Asparagus Risotto 47

Baked Veggies Risotto 47
Rice & Seafood Paella 48
Curried Chickpeas & Veggies 48
Beans & Quinoa with Veggies 49
Beans & Tomato Bake 49
Lentil Falafel Bowls 50

Chapter 8: Pasta, Couscous & Tagine Recipes 51
Pasta with Veggies 51
Four Cheese Pasta 51
Pasta with Beef 52
Pasta with Shrimp 52
Couscous & Veggie Bowl . 53
Couscous with Cauliflower & Dates 53
Couscous & Veggie Pilaf .. 54
Couscous Stuffed Bell Peppers 54
Veggie Tagine 55
Chicken Tagine 55

Chapter 9: Sandwiches, Pizzas & Wraps Recipes 56
Spinach & Tomato Sandwiches 56
Tuna Sandwiches 56
Peas & Feta Sandwiches .. 57

Zucchini Pizza 57
Four-Cheeses Pizza 58
Pepperoni Pizza 58
Chickpeas Wraps 59
Veggie Wraps 59
Chicken Wraps 60

Chapter 10: Sauces, Dips & Dressing Recipes 61
Basil Pesto Sauce 61
Marinara Sauce 61
Pizza Sauce 62
Yogurt Tzatziki Dip 62
Chickpeas Hummus 62
Eggplant Dip 63
Blue Cheese Dressing 63

Chapter 11: Fruits & Sweets Recipes 64
Poached Pears 64
Fruity Yogurt Parfait 64
Blueberry Gelato 65
Strawberry Zabaglione 65
Strawberry Crème Brûlée 66
Fig Cake 66
Apple Torte 67
Blueberry Clafoutis 67

90 Days Meal Plan 68

Conclusion 70

INTRODUCTION

The Mediterranean diet is defined by its flavor, color, and freshness. These three combined created a colorful selection of dishes on any dinner table. In terms of taste, this diet is the most varied, thanks to various herbs and spices. The freshness is enhanced by the combination of grains and legumes as well. Other than that, why is this diet so popular, and what do you need to do if you plan on sticking to this diet?

MEDITERRANEAN FOOD CULTURE THROUGH HISTORY

As the name suggests, this diet is designed by the inhabitants living along the Mediterranean Sea, from Spain to Morocco, through Tunisia, Greece, Italy, and other countries.

As you might expect, the Mediterranean diet has a long history. The name of the sea itself comes from the Latin "Mar Medi Terraneum", which translates into "sea in the middle of the land". A quick look at the map will tell you why they call it that way. In a way, it looks like an oversized pond.

Both culturally and historically, the Mediterranean basin is the birthplace and development of Western civilization. Its origins in Mesopotamia saw the growth and expansion of nations and empires such as Israel, Egypt, Phoenicia, Ancient Greece, and the Roman Empire.

The spread of Western civilization to the north and east during the Middle Ages and the irruption of Islam into the Mediterranean area led to the break-up of the unity of the Mediterranean. However, nations in the area continued to exchange commerce and culture despite religious and political differences.

Because of the wide variety of lifestyles, religions, and geography, the Mediterranean culinary heritage combines other cuisines such as North African, Ottoman, French, Spanish, Italian, Greek, etc.

WHAT IS THE MEDITERRANEAN DIET?

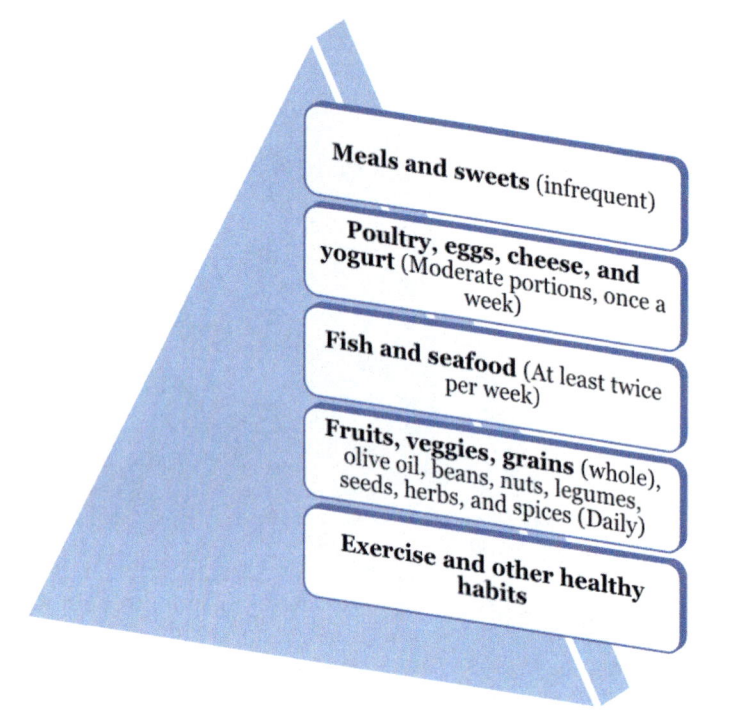

Meals and sweets (infrequent)

Poultry, eggs, cheese, and yogurt (Moderate portions, once a week)

Fish and seafood (At least twice per week)

Fruits, veggies, grains (whole), olive oil, beans, nuts, legumes, seeds, herbs, and spices (Daily)

Exercise and other healthy habits

The Mediterranean diet is based on traditional foods that people around the Mediterranean Sea ate back in the day, including Italy, Greece, Spain, and France. While there are no strict rules on what you can and cannot eat, it normally encourages the consumption of fruits, veggies, whole grains, legumes, nuts, seeds, and healthy fats. Ass for processed foods, added sugar, and refined grains, and limit or avoid them.

This diet is usually recommended for people who want to improve their health and reduce their risk of chronic diseases. The pyramid pictured above should give you a rough idea of what you need to eat and how often.

KEY HABITS TO FEEL HEALTHIER

The Mediterranean diet is only a piece of the puzzle, however. The Mediterranean lifestyle involves regular physical activities, sharing meals with friends and family, and minimizing stress levels.

With that in mind, here are some habits worth picking up to improve your overall health. It is worth noting that these will be useful regardless of your diet, so try your best to develop them.

Be More Active
Being physically active is more than just working out every other day. It also comes down to the little things you do every day. Fun fact: Mediterranean folks do not exercise that often. They do not spend hours at the gym daily, but many are fairly fit.

Just because they do not pump iron for hours on end does not mean that they are inactive. Nothing is super convenient in that part of the world, so people are just used to moving around naturally. They do a lot of manual labor. In other words, they use their legs when it comes to transportation. They're free, anyway.

So, in addition to working out, consider doing the following:
- Get up every hour: You can set a timer for this if you want, but at least try to get out of your seat every hour. Stand up and stretch. Maybe walk away from your computer or phone to clear your head. You can come back after a minute and feel refreshed, ready to take on whatever work you need.
- Take the stairs (if you're not in a hurry): Consider this an extra exercise. Taking the elevator is convenient, but you can get some small cardio done by taking the stairs. It'll also give you more time to think while you are going up.
- Walk: If your destination is not too far away, try walking instead of taking the bus or car. Weather permitting, walking anywhere under 10-15 minutes is a good distance. However, if all your destinations are far away, consider parking a bit further to get that walk-in.
- Do chores: Yes, doing housework is not the most exciting part of anyone's routine, but you cannot deny the positive psychological effect of a clean room, such as reducing depression, anxiety, and other negative emotions. A full hour of cleaning can also burn many calories, so consider it a form of exercise. One way to make chores more bearable is to play music while at it.
- Stretch: You do not need an hour-long yoga session at 6 in the morning to benefit from stretching. Instead, just a 10-minute long stretching session can improve circulation, limber your muscles, and set you up for a good day.

Dine With Others

The Mediterranean lifestyle also encourages you to dine with friends and family. There are many benefits to this, such as:

- Positive emotions: Communal meals are as old as humanity itself. When we eat together, our brain believes that we are safe and happy, releasing positive hormones and emotions. The University of Oxford pointed out that eating with others will make you overall happier with your life.
- Strengthen community: Dining with others also strengthens the bond between you. You would have time to share stories, laugh, and enjoy each other's company over a delicious Mediterranean meal. This is why wine and dine is still an effective means to build your network.
- Healthier eating: You eat slower when you are with others. Your body takes a while to understand that it is full, which will signal to the brain. If you eat too quickly, you will be overeating by the time you feel full. When you eat slowly, you give your body enough time to measure your fullness so that you would feel full without overeating.
- Healthier food choices: Studies have shown that adults also tend to make healthier food choices when in a group. We tend to reach out to that salad and fruits than crisps and soda when we are in the company of others. So, if you cook for a big group, incorporate healthy dishes, and people will go for it.
- Different atmosphere: The overall atmosphere is also different when you eat with your family. But you might have a get-together in a steak house or other locations you would not normally take yourself to if you were alone. You can sit back, relax, listen to music, and take in the atmosphere that only comes by when you spend quality time with your friends or family.

Manage Your Stress

Although the Mediterranean lifestyle appears energetic and colorful, it also respects that everybody needs to slow down and relax once in a while. With that in mind, here are some ways you can manage your stress:

- Exercise: It goes without saying, but working out regularly is one of the best ways to relax your mind and body.
- Deep breaths: This can quickly calm you down in a stressful situation. Just distance yourself from the situation, sit or lie down, close your eyes, and take a few deep breaths. Make sure to breathe using your diaphragm, meaning that your stomach should move, not your shoulders. Do this for a few minutes up to 10 if you need to. You will feel much better.
- Take a break: This requires a bit of time management. Break a major task into bite-sized chunks, tackle them one at a time, and take a short break between them. You can spend a few minutes outside, meditate, listen to music, etc. Yes, you want to get that job done quickly, but if you interject it with well-timed breaks, you will have more energy and focus on finishing the job, not to mention making fewer mistakes and feeling overall better throughout the process.
- Pick up hobbies: Spend some time doing the things you truly enjoy, such as reading, doing puzzles, watching a movie, playing golf, making art, etc. Just 15 to 20 minutes is enough if you are short on time. Also, it will help relieve stress.
- Talk about your problems: The Mediterranean lifestyle encourages a meaningful connection between people. When things get rough, you can turn to your friends and family for emotional support. Everybody needs to hear "You can do this" once in a while from someone they care about. Also, keep up your sense of humor because laughter goes a long way.

Live Simply

Although not completely by choice, the people of the Mediterranean usually have far fewer possessions than the United States. Due to their economic circumstances, they usually need to make do with what they have. That means they make smart decisions when it comes to daily needs.

When it comes to food, they usually do not buy ingredients in bulk. While it is indeed cheaper to buy in bulk, they also value freshness. Yes, that also means more frequent to the grocery store, but that is a good excuse to squeeze some walking in there.

There is also a great emphasis on social connections. Again, people keep things simple over there. Instead of having hundreds of "friends" whose names you can barely remember, the Mediterranean lifestyle encourages you to cultivate meaningful relationships with a few people you consider your friends.

Having a balanced social life and a true connection to the people who matter are helpful for your mental health, especially when the going gets tough.

Work Out

Let's be honest here. Everybody knows the benefits of an active lifestyle. Among them are weight control, improved heart health, elevated mood, and energy level. That said, going active might be difficult for some people, especially after recent global events. But it is never too late to start working out again.

Ideally, you go to the gym and have a personal trainer to help you get back on track, but not everybody is that committed. We all want easier alternatives, and going to the gym can be an intimidating experience for many people. Luckily, you do not even need to go to the gym to work out. You can start getting fit in the comfort of your own home.

Now, the first excuse people will say to avoid a workout is that they "don't have time". No one has enough time for anything. Everybody has 24 hours, but you do not see Bill Gates working out to be a world-class bodybuilder. The fact is that it is not a question of time but priorities.

Elon Musk didn't climb Mount Everest, not because he didn't have enough time, but because it wasn't important enough for him. So, you need to shift your mindset here. Is your health important enough for you to make some time to take care of it?

If time investment is a major problem for you, here's something to consider. You only need to work out 5 minutes at a time, maybe 3 times per week. Anyone can invest 15 minutes per week, right?

This is one reason why you should try HIIT or High-Intensity Interval Training. The idea is to go flat out in short bursts and take short breaks for a certain period. It can be just 5 minutes or 30, depending on how much time you can spare.

The benefit you get from 5 minutes of high-intensity exercise is far better than half-heartedly working out for an hour on your mat. The best part? You don't even need any equipment for it.

So, go on YouTube and look up a 5-minute HIIT exercise for beginners. It will be over before you know it, and you might even crave more. You can do it every day if you want, but 3 times a week would be enough. Start here, then work your way up to 15 minutes of HIIT. At that point, you might develop an interest in hitting the gym. Even if you don't, you are already more fit than most of your friends at this point.

WHY IS THIS DIET FAMOUS AND ITS POTENTIAL BENEFITS

There are a few reasons why the Mediterranean diet is so popular. The biggest factor is the fact that this diet has proven health benefits. Many studies have been done on this diet, and it is pretty well-known that it is very healthy. It uses all sorts of healthy foodstuffs that lead to higher life expectancy and quality of health in the long run.

Moreover, this diet is very flexible. Many other diets fail because they impose restrictions on certain foods or even the entire food group. This is not sustainable for many people. For the Mediterranean diet, the most you need to limit your intake so you are not removing anything. It just replaces it with healthier alternatives.

Another reason why people love this diet so much is that it is not only about weight loss. It is intended to add a bit of spice to your life and help you lead a healthier life.

Potential Benefits
The Mediterranean diet has many benefits, such as:

Promotes Heart Health
Many studies have been done on a diet to understand its ability to promote heart health. They all agree that this diet may be linked to a lower risk of stroke and heart disease.
One such study looked into the effect of this diet compared to a low-fat diet and found that the Mediterranean diet is more effective at slowing the development of plaque buildup in the arteries, which is a huge risk factor for heart disease.
Another study also found that the Mediterranean diet can lower systolic and diastolic blood pressure levels to support heart health.

Maintain Healthy Blood Sugar Levels
Because the Mediterranean diet contains a lot of nutrient-dense foods, it can help stabilize your blood sugar levels. As a result, it helps lower the risk of developing type 2 diabetes. Multiple studies have shown that this diet can improve levels of hemoglobin A1C, which is a marker used to measure long-term blood sugar control. They also found that the Mediterranean diet can lower fasting blood sugar levels.
In addition, this diet has been shown to lower insulin resistance. This condition inhibits the body's ability to use insulin to control blood sugar levels effectively.

Protect Brain Function
Many studies also show that the Mediterranean diet can aid in rain health and protect against cognitive decline when you get holder.
One study involving 512 people on this diet showed that those who adhere to the Mediterranean diet had better memory and fewer risk factors for Alzheimer's disease. Another study found that this diet is linked to a lower risk of dementia and cognitive impairment.
One large review of this diet also found that it is linked to improved cognitive function, attention, memory, and processing speed among healthy older adults.

WHAT TO EAT AND WHAT TO LIMIT

There is no strict eating time or pattern for the Mediterranean diet and what foods belong in the Mediterranean diet is a controversial topic. This is because no one can agree on what counts. After all, there are so many variations between countries. However, we have a good idea of what you should and should not have on your plate, which we will discuss in this section.

Foods to Eat
Your diet should be based on these:

- Veggies: Broccoli, cucumbers, cauliflower, carrots, Brussels sprout, sweet potatoes, potatoes, tomatoes, kale, spinach, onions, turnips
- Fruits: Peaches, melons, figs, dates, grapes, strawberries, pears, oranges, bananas, apples
- Nuts, seeds, and nut butter: walnuts, almonds, macadamia nuts, cashews, hazelnuts, pumpkin seeds, sunflower seeds, almond butter, peanut butter
- Legumes: chickpeas, peanuts, pulses, lentils, peas, beans
- Whole grains: Whole wheat bread and pasta, buckwheat, corn, barley, rye, brown rice, oats
- Fish and seafood: mussels, crabs, clams, oysters, shrimps, mackerels, tunas, trout, sardines, salmons
- Poultry: Turkey, chicken, duck
- Eggs: Chicken, duck, and quail eggs

- Dairy: Milk, cheese, yogurt
- Herbs and spices: pepper, cinnamon, nutmeg, sage, rosemary, mint, basil, garlic
- Healthy fats: avocados, avocado oil, olives, and extra virgin olive oil

Foods to Limit
When following the Mediterranean diet, do your best to avoid or at least limit the following:

- Added sugar: Found in many foods, but great quantity in ice cream, candies, soda, table sugar, syrup, and baked goods
- Refined grains: Crackers, chips, tortillas, pasta, white bread
- Trans fat: Found in fried foods, margarine, and other processed foods
- Refined oils: Grapeseed oil, cottonseed oil, canola oil, soybean oil
- Processed meat: Hotdogs, deli meat, beef jerky, processed sausages
- Highly processed foods: Fast foods, convenience meals, granola bars, microwave popcorn

What About Beverages?
Stick to water. The diet also incorporates a moderate amount of red wine – about a daily glass. You can skip the alcohol completely if you can help it. Anyone pregnant with trouble drinking in moderation or taking medication that can interact with alcohol should also avoid red wine altogether.

Okay, but what about coffee and tea? Good news, you can have those as well. Just watch what you put into your tea and coffee. Avoid sugar or cream.

Limit your consumption of sugar-sweetened beverages like soda or sweet tea, both of which have a lot of added sugar. You can drink fruit juice in moderation, but you should go for whole fruits for the benefit of fiber.

Snack Options
If you are moving away from a calorie-rich diet to the Mediterranean diet, you could get hungry between meals. Instead of grabbing that bag of chips, consider these healthier alternatives:

- Cottage cheese with fresh fruit
- Sliced bell peppers with guacamole
- Apple slices with almond butter
- Hard-boiled egg with salt and pepper
- Greek yogurt
- Baby carrots with hummus
- Some nuts
- A piece of fruit
- Mixed berries
- Grapes

MEASUREMENT CONVERSION TABLE

To aid you in your cooking, here are 3 conversion tables based on measurement, temperature, and weight for both imperial and metric systems. NOTE: The decimals are rounded.

Volumes

Cup	Fluid ounces (Oz)	Milliliters (ml)	Teaspoons
8	64	1895	128
6	48	1420	96
5	40	1180	80
4	32	960	64
2	16	480	32
1	8	240	16
3/4	6	177	12
2/3	5	158	11
1/2	4	118	8
3/8	3	90	6
1/3	2.5	79	5.5
1/4	2	59	4
1/8	1	30	3
1/16	1/2	15	1

Temperature

Fahrenheit (°F)	Celsius (°C)
100	37
150	65
200	93
250	121
300	150
325	160
350	180
375	190
400	200
425	220
450	230
500	260
525	274
550	288

Weight

Ounce (oz)	Gram (g)
1/2	15
1	29
2	57
3	85
4	113
5	141
6	170
8	227
10	283
12	340
13	369
14	397
15	425

Pound (lbs)	Gram (g)
1	454
2	907
3	1,361
4	1,814
5	2,268
6	2,722
7	31,75
8	3,629
9	4,082
10	4,536

CHAPTER 1:
Breakfast Recipes

YOGURT WITH CARAMELIZED FIGS

Serves: 4 individuals | Preparation Time: 10 minutes

Ingredients:
- 3 tablespoons honey, divided
- 8 ounces fresh figs, halved
- 2 cups plain Greek yogurt
- ¼ cup pistachios, chopped

Directions:
1. In a medium-sized wok, add 1 tablespoon of the honey over medium heat and cook for about 1-2 minutes or until heated.
2. In the wok, place the figs, cut sides down and cook for about 5 minutes or until caramelized.
3. Remove the wok of figs from the heat and set aside for about 2-3 minutes.
4. Divide the yogurt into serving bowls evenly and top each with the caramelized fig halves.
5. Sprinkle with pistachios.
6. Drizzle each bowl with the remaining honey and serve.

Nutritional Information per Serving:
Calories: 296, Fat: 3.8g, Net Carbohydrates: 52.8g, Carbohydrates: 58.8g, Fiber: 6g, Sugar: 49g, Protein: 9.7g, Sodium: 112mg

YOGURT OATMEAL

Serves: 4 individuals | Preparation Time: 10 minutes | Cooking Time: 10 minutes

Ingredients:
- 2 cups water
- 1 cup old-fashioned oats
- 2 tablespoons tahini
- 1 tablespoon honey
- 1 tablespoon fresh lemon juice
- ¼ teaspoon ground allspice
- 1 (7-ounce) container of plain Greek yogurt
- ¼ teaspoon ground cinnamon
- 4 tablespoons fresh blueberries
- 2 tablespoons pistachios, chopped

Directions:
1. Add the water over medium heat in a saucepan and cook until boiling.
2. Stir in the oats and cook for about 5 minutes, stirring occasionally.
3. Meanwhile, for the sauce: in a small-sized blender, add the tahini, honey, lemon juice and allspice and pulse until smooth.
4. Remove the pan of oats from the heat and stir half the yogurt and cinnamon.
5. Divide the oatmeal into serving bowls evenly.
6. Top each bowl with the remaining yogurt, followed by the blueberries and pistachios.
7. Drizzle with the tahini sauce and serve.

Nutritional Information per Serving:
Calories: 375, Fat: 14.2g, Net Carbohydrates: 44.5g, Carbohydrates: 50g, Fiber: 6.5g, Sugar: 18.9g, Protein: 14.2g, Sodium: 109mg

AVOCADO & EGGS TOAST

Serves: 4 individuals | Preparation Time: 10 minutes | Cooking Time: 8 minutes

Ingredients:
- 1 large avocado, peeled, pitted and roughly chopped
- ¼ teaspoon fresh lemon juice
- 2 tablespoons fresh mint leaves, finely chopped
- Salt and ground black pepper, as required
- 4 large rye bread slices
- 4 hard-boiled eggs, peeled and sliced
- 2 tablespoons feta cheese, crumbled

Directions:
1. Add the avocado to a bowl and, with a fork, mash roughly.
2. Add the lemon juice, mint, salt and black pepper and stir to combine well. Set aside.
3. Heat a non-stick frying pan over medium-high heat and toast 1 bread slice for about 2 minutes per side.
4. Repeat with the remaining slices.
5. Spread the avocado mixture over each slice evenly.
6. Sprinkle with feta and serve immediately.

Nutritional Information per Serving:
Calories: 197, Fat: 15.4g, Net Carbohydrates: 4.5g, Carbohydrates: 8.5g, Fiber: 4g, Sugar: 1.1g, Protein: 7.9g, Sodium: 203mg

YOGURT WAFFLES

Serves: 6 individuals | Preparation Time: 10 minutes | Cooking Time: 30 minutes

Ingredients:
- 2 cups all-purpose flour
- 1 tablespoon plus 2 teaspoons baking powder
- 1 teaspoon ground cinnamon
- Pinch of ground nutmeg
- Pinch of ground cloves
- ¼ teaspoon salt
- 2 large eggs
- 1¼ cups milk
- 2/3 cup plain Greek yogurt
- 2 teaspoons honey
- 1 teaspoon vanilla extract
- Olive oil cooking spray

Directions:
1. In a medium-sized bowl, blend the flour, baking powder, spices and salt.
2. In another large-sized bowl, add the remaining ingredients and whisk until well blended.
3. Add the flour mixture and mix until well blended and smooth.
4. Preheat the waffle iron and then grease it with cooking spray.
5. Place 1/3-½ cup of the mixture into preheated waffle iron and cook for about 4-5 minutes or until golden brown.
6. Repeat with the remaining mixture. Serve warm.

Nutritional Information per Serving:
Calories: 234, Fat: 3.5g, Net Carbohydrates: 39g, Carbohydrates: 40.4g, Fiber: 1.4g, Sugar: 6.5g, Protein: 9.7g, Sodium: 168mg

RICOTTA PANCAKES

Serves: 4 individuals | Preparation Time: 10 minutes | Cooking Time: 20 minutes

Ingredients:
- Olive oil cooking spray
- 4 eggs
- ½ cup ricotta cheese
- ¼ cup unsweetened vanilla whey protein powder
- ½ teaspoon baking powder
- Pinch of salt
- ½ teaspoon liquid stevia
- 2 tablespoons unsalted butter

Directions:
1. Add all the ingredients and pulse until well combined in a clean blender.
2. In a non-stick wok, melt the butter over medium heat.
3. Add the desired amount of mixture and spread it evenly.
4. Cook for about 2-3 minutes or until golden brown.
5. Flip and cook for about 1-2 minutes or until golden brown.
6. Repeat with the remaining mixture. Serve warm.

Nutritional Information per Serving:
Calories: 186, Fat: 13g, Net Carbohydrates: 3.1g, Carbohydrates: 3.1g, Fiber: 0g, Sugar: 0.7g, Protein: 14.5g, Sodium: 194mg

MIXED VEGGIE MUFFINS

Serves: 8 individuals | Preparation Time: 15 minutes | Cooking Time: 12 minutes

Ingredients:
- Olive oil cooking spray
- ¼ cup half-and-half

- 6 large eggs
- Salt and ground black pepper, as required
- ½ cup sun-dried tomatoes in oil, drained and chopped
- 1/3 cup canned olives, drained, pitted, and quartered
- ¼ cup bottled sweet red peppers, drained and chopped
- ¼ cup canned artichokes in oil drained and thinly sliced
- ¼ cup Asiago cheese, shredded
- ¼ cup feta cheese, crumbled
- ¼ cup fresh parsley, chopped

Directions:
1. Preheat your oven to 375 °F.
2. Grease 24 cups of mini muffin tins with cooking spray.
3. In a bowl, add the half-and-half, eggs, salt and black pepper and whisk until well blended.
4. Add the vegetables and Asiago cheese to another large bowl and mix well.
5. Place the egg mixture into the prepared muffin cups about ¾ of full.
6. Place the vegetable mixture over the egg mixture evenly and top with the remaining.
7. Sprinkle each cup with feta and parsley evenly.
8. Bake for approximately 12 minutes or until the eggs are done completely.
9. Remove the muffin tin from the oven and place it onto a wire rack to cool for about 5 minutes.
10. Then invert the muffins onto a platter and serve warm.

Nutritional Information per Serving:
Calories: 103, Fat: 7.5g, Net Carbohydrates: 2g, Carbohydrates: 2.7g, Fiber: 0.7g, Sugar: 1g, Protein: 7g, Sodium: 208mg

MULTI-GRAIN BREAD

Serves: 20 individuals | Preparation Time: 15 minutes | Cooking Time: 30 minutes

Ingredients:
- ¼ cup rolled oats
- ¼ cup quinoa
- ¼ cup sunflower seeds
- ¼ cup cold water
- 1 tablespoon active yeast
- 3 cups warm water
- 4 cups all-purpose flour
- 1 cup whole-wheat flour
- 1 cup rye flour
- Olive oil cooking spray

Directions:
1. In a large-sized bowl, add the oats, quinoa, sunflower seeds, rolled oats, and cold water and mix until well blended.
2. With plastic wrap, cover the bowl of oat mixture and set aside at room temperature for 1 hour.
3. Place yeast and water in a separate large bowl and mix until dissolved completely. Let it rest for 5 minutes or until it begins to foam.
4. In the bowl of yeast mixture, add flour and quinoa mixture and mix until well blended.
5. With plastic wrap, cover the dough bowl and set aside at room temperature for 2 hours.
6. Remove the plastic wrap from the dough bowl and place it onto a lightly floured surface.
7. Divide the dough into two equal-sized balls.
8. Grease 2 loaf pans with cooking spray.
9. Place 1 dough ball in each prepared loaf pan and set aside, uncovered for 1 hour.
10. Preheat your oven to 450 °F.
11. Bake for approximately 26-30 minutes or until a wooden skewer inserted in the center comes out clean.
12. Remove the loaf pans from the oven and place them onto a wire rack to cool for about 10 minutes.
13. Now, invert each piece of bread onto the wire rack to cool completely before slicing.
14. Cut each bread loaf into desired-sized slices and serve.

Nutritional Information per Serving:
Calories: 155, Fat: 1.2g, Net Carbohydrates: 27.7g, Carbohydrates: 31.1g, Fiber: 3.4g, Sugar: 0.2g, Protein: 5.3g, Sodium: 1mg

POTATO OMELET

Serves: 4 individuals | Preparation Time: 10 minutes | Cooking Time: 15 minutes

Ingredients:
- ½ cup olive oil
- ½ pounds potatoes, thinly sliced
- Salt and ground black pepper, as required
- 1 large onion, thinly sliced
- 4 eggs
- 2 tomatoes, peeled, seeded and roughly chopped

- 2 scallions, chopped

Directions:
1. In a large-sized wok, heat the oil over medium-high heat and cook the potatoes with a little salt and black pepper for about 3-4 minutes or until golden brown and crisp.
2. Stir in the onion and cook for about 5 minutes, stirring occasionally.
3. Meanwhile, in a bowl, add the eggs, salt and black pepper and beat well.
4. Add the egg mixture into the wok with the potato mixture and gently stir to combine.
5. Now, adjust the heat to low and cook until the eggs begin to set on the bottom.
6. With a spatula, Carefully flip the omelet and cook until the eggs are set.
7. Serve warm with the garnishing of tomato and scallion.

Nutritional Information per Serving:
Calories: 347, Fat: 29.8g, Net Carbohydrates: 12.6g, Carbohydrates: 15.7g, Fiber: 3.1g, Sugar: 4.4g, Protein: 7.6g, Sodium: 71mg

SHAKSHUKA

Serves: 4 individuals | Preparation Time: 15 minutes | Cooking Time: 50 minutes

Ingredients:
- 2 tablespoons olive oil
- 4 small yellow onions, sliced
- ½ cup tomato, finely chopped
- 1 garlic clove, minced
- 4 large eggs
- 3 ounces feta cheese, crumbled
- Salt and ground black pepper, as required
- 2 tablespoons fresh dill, minced

Directions:
1. In a large-sized cast-iron wok, melt heat oil over medium-low heat and stir in the onions, spreading in an even layer.
2. Now, adjust the heat to low and cook for about 30 minutes, stirring every 5-10 minutes.
3. Add the tomato and garlic and cook for about 2-3 minutes, stirring frequently.
4. With the spoon, spread the mixture in an even layer.
5. Carefully crack the eggs over the onion mixture and sprinkle with the feta cheese, salt, and black pepper.
6. Cover the wok tightly and cook for about 10-15 minutes or until the desired doneness of the eggs.
7. Serve hot with the garnishing of parsley.

Nutritional Information per Serving:
Calories: 217, Fat: 10.1g, Net Carbohydrates: 8.1g, Carbohydrates: 10.1g, Fiber: 2g, Sugar: 5.1g, Protein: 10.8g, Sodium: 396mg

HAM QUICHE

Serves: 6 individuals | Preparation Time: 15 minutes | Cooking Time: 40 minutes

Ingredients:
- 5 eggs
- ½ cup half-and-half
- 2 teaspoons garlic, chopped
- Ground black pepper, as required
- 1 (9-inch) refrigerated pie crust, thawed
- 1 (4-ounce) package tomato-basil feta cheese, crumbled
- ¼ cup red onion, finely chopped
- ½ cup cooked ham, chopped
- 2 cups baby spinach leaves, roughly chopped
- ½ cup roasted red peppers, drained and chopped
- ½ cup mozzarella cheese, shredded

Directions:
1. Preheat your oven to 375 °F.
2. In a small-sized bowl, add the eggs, half-and-half, garlic and black pepper and whisk until well blended.
3. Arrange the pie crust in a 9-inch quiche pan and sprinkle with feta cheese evenly.
4. Place the onion and ham over the cheese, followed by spinach and red peppers.
5. Place the egg mixture on top and sprinkle with mozzarella cheese.
6. Bake for approximately 35-40 minutes or until a wooden skewer inserted in the center comes out clean.
7. Remove the quiche pan from the oven and place it onto a wire rack for about 5 minutes before slicing.
8. Cut into desired-sized wedges and serve.

Nutritional Information per Serving:
Calories: 306, Fat: 18.7g, Net Carbohydrates: 22.3g, Carbohydrates: 23.4g, Fiber: 1.1g, Sugar: 13.1g, Protein: 12.2g, Sodium: 642mg

CHAPTER 2:
Meze, Antipasti & Appetizer Recipes

CUCUMBER & WALNUT PLATTER

Serves: 10 individuals | Preparation Time: 20 minutes | Cooking Time: 4 minutes

Ingredients:
- 1 cup walnuts
- 1 pound Persian cucumbers, sliced
- ¾ teaspoon salt, divided
- 2 tablespoons fresh basil, shredded and divided
- 1 garlic clove, crushed
- ½ teaspoon lemon zest, grated
- 1 tablespoon extra-virgin olive oil
- ½ teaspoon ground pepper
- 3 cups plain Greek yogurt, whipped
- 2 tablespoons butter

Directions:
1. Soak the walnuts for about 5 hours in a large bowl of water.
2. Drain the walnuts and rinse them under cold running water.
3. Again, place the walnuts in a bowl of fresh water and refrigerate overnight.
4. Again, drain the walnuts and pat them dry with paper towels.
5. Then chop the walnuts roughly. Set aside.
6. In a large-sized bowl, place the cucumber slices and sprinkle with ¼ teaspoon of salt.
7. With a potato masher, mash the cucumbers until juicy.
8. Place the mashed cucumber in a colander and set aside to drain for about 5 minutes.
9. Transfer the drained cucumber into a large-sized bowl and stir in 1 tablespoon of basil, garlic, lemon zest, oil, black pepper and remaining salt.
10. Place the yogurt onto a serving platter and top with the cucumber mixture and walnuts.
11. In a small-sized wok, melt the butter over medium heat for about 2-4 minutes, stirring continuously.
12. Immediately remove the wok from the heat and drizzle over the cucumbers.
13. Serve with the garnishing of remaining basil.

Nutritional Information per Serving:
Calories: 170, Fat: 12g, Net Carbohydrates: 7.2g, Carbohydrates: 8.3g, Fiber: 1.1g, Sugar: 6.1g, Protein: 7.6g, Sodium: 244mg

TAHINI POTATO PLATTER

Serves: 6 individuals | Preparation Time: 15 minutes | Cooking Time: 20 minutes

Ingredients:
- 3 pounds small new potatoes, scrubbed

- Salt, as required
- 1 bunch of fresh cilantro, roughly chopped
- ½ cup tahini
- ¼ cup fresh lemon juice
- 2 tablespoons water
- 2 tablespoons fresh parsley, chopped
- 2 teaspoons extra-virgin olive oil

Directions:
1. Add the potatoes over high heat in a large saucepan of salted water and cook until boiling.
2. Now, adjust the heat to low and simmer for about 15 minutes.
3. Remove the pan of potatoes from heat and set aside to cool to room temperature in the water for about 1½-2 hours.
4. Drain the potatoes and cut each in half.
5. Transfer the potatoes to a large-sized bowl.
6. In a clean blender, add the cilantro, tahini, lemon juice and water and pulse until well blended and smooth.
7. In the bowl of potatoes, add the potatoes, parsley, salt and tahini mixture and toss to coat well.
8. Transfer the potato mixture onto a platter and drizzle with oil.
9. Serve immediately.

Nutritional Information per Serving:
Calories: 292, Fat: 12.6g, Net Carbohydrates: 32.8g, Carbohydrates: 40.2g, Fiber: 7.4g, Sugar: 2.9g, Protein: 7.3g, Sodium: 67mg

TABBOULEH PLATTER

Serves: 3 individuals | Preparation Time: 15 minutes

Ingredients:
- ½ cup uncooked bulgur
- 2 cups hot vegetable broth
- 2-3 Roma tomatoes, cored and chopped
- 2-3 cups fresh Italian flat-leaf parsley, chopped
- ½ cup fresh mint, chopped
- ¼ cup scallions, chopped
- 2 tablespoons olive oil
- 2 tablespoons fresh lemon juice
- ½ teaspoon salt

Directions:
1. In a large-sized bowl, add the bulgur and broth and set aside, covered for about 30-60 minutes or until softened.
2. Through a fine-mesh strainer, strain the bulgur and transfer it into a large-sized serving bowl.
3. In the bowl of bulgur, add the remaining ingredients and mix until well combined.
4. Serve immediately.

Nutritional Information per Serving:
Calories: 226, Fat: 11.2g, Net Carbohydrates: 18.2g, Carbohydrates: 26.1g, Fiber: 7.9g, Sugar: 3.5g, Protein: 8.7g, Sodium: 935mg

ANTIPASTI LAYERED DIP

Serves: 12 individuals | Preparation Time: 20 minutes

Ingredients:
- 1 (15-ounce) can of cannellini beans
- 2 tablespoons extra-virgin olive oil, divided
- 1½ teaspoons Italian seasoning
- ¼ teaspoon garlic powder
- Salt and ground black pepper, as required
- ½ cup cream cheese, softened
- ¼ cup part-skim ricotta cheese
- 1 teaspoon fresh lemon juice
- ½ cup canned artichoke hearts, chopped
- ½ cup tomatoes, chopped
- ¼ cup Pecorino Romano cheese, grated
- ¼ cup fresh basil leaves, torn
- ¼ cup salami, sliced
- 3 tablespoons pepperoncini rings

Directions:
1. Drain the can of beans, reserving 2 tablespoons of liquid.
2. Rinse the beans and drain well.
3. In a large-sized bowl, add the beans, reserved liquid, 1 tablespoon of oil, Italian seasoning, garlic powder, salt and black pepper and with a potato masher, mash until smooth.
4. Transfer the mashed beans mixture into a 9-inch pie dish and spread in an even layer.
5. In a small-sized bowl, add the cream cheese, ricotta, lemon juice and remaining salt and black pepper and whisk until smooth.
6. Spread the cheese mixture on top of the bean layer.

7. Spread the artichokes and tomatoes over the cheese mixture evenly.
8. Top with Romano cheese, followed by basil, salami and pepperoncini evenly.
9. Drizzle with the remaining oil and serve.

Nutritional Information per Serving:
Calories: 202, Fat: 8g, Net Carbohydrates: 13.7g, Carbohydrates: 22.9g, Fiber: 9.2g, Sugar: 1.2g, Protein: 11g, Sodium: 208mg

DELI MEAT ANTIPASTI

Serves: 8 individuals | Preparation Time: 15 minutes

Ingredients:
- 24 salami slices
- 16 parma ham slices
- 16 mortadella slices
- 1 pound mozzarella cheese, cubed
- 16 olives
- 16 cornichons
- 16 radishes
- 4 tablespoons olive oil
- Ground black pepper, as required

Directions:
1. Arrange all ingredients onto a serving platter and serve immediately.

Nutritional Information per Serving:
Calories: 341, Fat: 29.1g, Net Carbohydrates: 3.1g, Carbohydrates: 5.8g, Fiber: 2.7g, Sugar: 0.7g, Protein: 16.1g, Sodium: 1913mg

DELI MEAT & VEGGIE ANTIPASTI

Serves: 20 individuals | Preparation Time: 20 minutes

Ingredients:
- 1 pound bocconcini
- 1½ tablespoons extra-virgin olive oil
- 1 tablespoon fresh flat-leaf parsley, chopped
- ½ teaspoon red pepper flakes, crushed
- Salt and ground black pepper, as required
- 2 large radicchio heads, separated into leaves
- 1 pound provolone cheese, cubed
- 1 pound Pecorino cheese, cubed
- ¾ pound salami, thinly sliced
- ¾ pound prosciutto, very thinly sliced
- ¾ pound refrigerator-dried soppressata, thinly sliced
- ¾ pound air-dried soppressata, thinly sliced
- 2 cups roasted red peppers, drained and sliced
- 2 cups artichoke hearts, drained and quartered
- 2 cups pepperoncini, drained
- 2 cups mixed olives, drained
- 10 fresh figs, halved lengthwise

Directions:
1. In a large-sized bowl, blend the bocconcini, olive oil, parsley, and red pepper flakes. , salt and black pepper. Set aside.
2. Line a large serving platter with radicchio leaves.
3. Arrange the remaining ingredients over radicchio leaves.
4. Top with bocconcini mixture and serve.

Nutritional Information per Serving:
Calories: 559, Fat: 39.6g, Net Carbohydrates: 11.2g, Carbohydrates: 13.8g, Fiber: 2.6g, Sugar: 6.1g, Protein: 37.4g, Sodium: 1977mg

TOASTED RAVIOLI

Serves: 8 individuals | Preparation Time: 15 minutes | Cooking Time: 12 minutes

Ingredients:
- 1 cup all-purpose flour
- 2 eggs
- ¼ cup water
- 1 cup breadcrumbs
- 1 teaspoon Italian seasoning
- 1 teaspoon garlic salt
- 16 ounces of meat ravioli
- 1-2 cups olive oil

Directions:
1. In a shallow dish, place the flour.

2. Place the eggs and water in a second shallow dish and beat well.
3. Mix the breadcrumbs, Italian seasoning, and garlic salt in a third shallow dish.
4. Coat each ravioli in flour, dip in the egg mixture, and coat with the breadcrumbs mixture.
5. In a deep wok, heat the oil over medium heat and fry the ravioli in 4 batches for about 3 minutes or until golden brown, flipping occasionally.
6. Transfer the fried ravioli onto a paper towel-lined plate with a slotted spoon to drain.
7. Serve warm.

Nutritional Information per Serving:
Calories: 416, Fat: 29.9g, Net Carbohydrates: 31.7g, Carbohydrates: 33.7g, Fiber: 2g, Sugar: 1.1g, Protein: 8.3g, Sodium: 261mg

7. Stir in the tomatoes, dried herbs, sugar and black pepper and cook until boiling.
8. Now, adjust the heat to low and simmer for about 40-45 minutes or until the sauce becomes slightly thick, stirring occasionally.
9. Meanwhile, in a large-sized wok, heat the remaining oil over medium heat and cook the cheese slices in 4 batches for about 30-60 seconds per side or until golden brown.
10. With a slotted spoon, transfer the fried mozzarella sticks onto a paper towel-lined plate to drain.
11. Serve warm alongside the sauce.

Nutritional Information per Serving:
Calories: 150, Fat: 7.9g, Net Carbohydrates: 13.2g, Carbohydrates: 15.8g, Fiber: 2.6g, Sugar: 4.5g, Protein: 4.7g, Sodium: 239mg

FRIED MOZZARELLA

Serves: 12 individuals | Preparation Time: 20 minutes | Cooking Time: 50 minutes

Ingredients:
- 1 pound part-skim mozzarella cheese
- 2 eggs, beaten
- 2/3 cup all-purpose flour
- ¾ cup seasoned breadcrumbs
- ¼ cup plus 1 tablespoon olive oil, divided
- 1 garlic clove, minced
- 1 (28-ounce) can of crushed tomatoes
- 1 teaspoon dried oregano, crushed
- ¼ teaspoon dried basil, crushed
- 2 teaspoons sugar
- 1/8 teaspoon ground black pepper

Directions:
1. Cut the mozzarella cheese into 24 (¼-inch) slices.
2. Place the eggs, flour and breadcrumbs in three shallow dishes respectively.
3. Dip each cheese slice in eggs, then coat with flour.
4. Again, dip cheese slices in eggs and then coat with breadcrumbs.
5. Arrange the mozzarella sticks onto waxed paper-lined baking sheets in a single layer and refrigerate for at least 1 hour.
6. For the sauce: in a small-sized saucepan, heat 1 tablespoon oil over medium heat and sauté the garlic for about 1 minute.

STUFFED MUSHROOMS

Serves: 4 individuals | Preparation Time: 20 minutes | Cooking Time: 45 minutes

Ingredients:
- Olive oil cooking spray
- 6 ounces clams
- 1 tablespoon butter, softened
- 1 tablespoon scallion, finely chopped
- ½ teaspoon garlic, minced
- 1 teaspoon dried oregano
- 1/8 teaspoon garlic salt
- ½ cup Italian breadcrumbs
- 1 egg, beaten
- ¼ cup plus 2 tablespoons mozzarella cheese, grated and divided
- 2 tablespoons Parmesan cheese, grated
- 1 tablespoon Romano cheese, grated
- ¼ cup butter, melted
- 8 mushrooms, stems removed
- 2 tablespoons fresh parsley, chopped

Directions:
1. Preheat your oven to 350 ºF.
2. Grease a baking dish with cooking spray.
3. Drain the clams well, reserving the liquid in a bowl.
4. Add the clams, softened butter, scallion, garlic, oregano and garlic salt in a bowl and mix well.
5. Add the reserved clam juice, breadcrumbs, and egg and mix until well combined.

6. Add 2 tablespoons of mozzarella, Parmesan and Romano cheese and mix well.
7. Arrange the mushrooms onto a platter and stuff each cavity with a clam mixture.
8. Arrange the mushrooms in the prepared baking dish and drizzle with melted butter.
9. Bake for approximately 35-40 minutes.
10. Remove from the oven and sprinkle the mushrooms with the remaining mozzarella cheese.
11. Bake for approximately 5 minutes or until the cheese is just slightly melted.
12. Garnish with parsley and serve.

Nutritional Information per Serving:
Calories: 362, Fat: 24.9g, Net Carbohydrates: 16.4g, Carbohydrates: 17.8g, Fiber: 1.4g, Sugar: 3.1g, Protein: 18.4g, Sodium: 665mg

Nutritional Information per Serving:
Calories: 492, Fat: 30.2g, Net Carbohydrates: 6g, Carbohydrates: 6.8g, Fiber: 0.8g, Sugar: 1.9g, Protein: 48.1g, Sodium: 585mg

TUNA CROQUETTES

Serves: 4 individuals | Preparation Time: 15 minutes | Cooking Time: 16 minutes

Ingredients:
- 24 ounces canned white tuna, drained
- ¼ cup mayonnaise
- 4 large eggs
- 2 tablespoons yellow onion, finely chopped
- 1 scallion, thinly sliced
- 4 garlic cloves, minced
- ¾ cup almond flour
- Salt and ground black pepper, as required
- ¼ cup olive oil

Directions:
1. In a large-sized bowl, place the tuna, mayonnaise, eggs, onion, scallion, garlic, almond flour, salt, and black pepper and mix until well combined.
2. Make 8 equal-sized oblong-shaped patties from the mixture.
3. Heat the olive oil over medium-high heat in a large-sized wok and fry the croquettes in 2 batches for about 2-4 minutes per side.
4. Transfer the croquettes onto a paper towel-lined plate with a slotted spoon to drain completely.
5. Serve warm.

CHAPTER 3:
Salads & Soups Recipes

CHICKEN SALAD

Serves: 6 individuals | Preparation Time: 15 minutes

Ingredients:
For Salad:
- 3 cups cooked chicken breast, cubed
- 2 cups tomatoes, chopped
- 1 cup Kalamata olives, pitted
- ½ cup red onion, finely chopped
- ½ cup feta cheese, crumbled

For Dressing:
- ¼ cup extra-virgin olive oil
- 2 tablespoons fresh lemon juice
- 1 tablespoon fresh cilantro, minced
- Salt and ground black pepper, as required

Directions:
1. For the salad: in a large-sized salad bowl, mix all ingredients.
2. For the dressing, add all the ingredients in a small bowl and beat until well combined.
3. Place the dressing over the salad and toss to coat well.
4. Refrigerate to chill completely before serving.

Nutritional Information per Serving:
Calories: 251, Fat: 15.7g, Net Carbohydrates: 3.6g, Carbohydrates: 5.3g, Fiber: 1.7g, Sugar: 2.6g, Protein: 22.9g, Sodium: 410mg

STEAK SALAD

Serves: 6 individuals | Preparation Time: 20 minutes | Cooking Time: 10 minutes

Ingredients:
- Olive oil cooking spray

For Steak:
- 1½ pounds aged rump steak, trimmed
- Salt and ground black pepper, as required
- 2 tablespoons olive oil

For Dressing:
- ½ cup mayonnaise
- 2 tablespoons plain yogurt
- 1 teaspoon Dijon mustard
- 1 tablespoon fresh lime juice
- 2 large green chilies, finely chopped
- 10 anchovies, chopped
- Salt and ground black pepper, as required

For Salad:
- 3 cups green olives, pitted and sliced
- 2 tablespoons fresh lime zest, grated
- 2 tablespoons fresh parsley, chopped
- 2 tablespoons fresh mint, chopped
- 4 tablespoons olive oil

Directions:
1. Preheat your grill to medium-high heat.
2. Grease the grill grate with cooking spray.

3. Sprinkle the beef steak with salt and black pepper generously, then drizzle with oil.
4. Place the steak onto the grill and cook for about 5 minutes per side.
5. Remove the steak from the grill and place it on a cutting board for about 10 minutes before slicing.
6. Cut the steak into desired-sized slices diagonally across the grain.
7. Add all the ingredients and mix well for dressing in a bowl.
8. Add the steak slices and stir to combine.
9. For the salad, add the olives, lime zest and herbs in another small bowl and mix.
10. Divide the steak mixture onto serving plates and top with the olives mixture.
11. Drizzle with oil and serve.

Nutritional Information per Serving:
Calories: 598, Fat: 44.7g, Net Carbohydrates: 2.7g, Carbohydrates: 5.3g, Fiber: 2.6g, Sugar: 0.5g, Protein: 45.8g, Sodium: 1500mg

CHICKPEAS SALAD

Serves: 8 individuals | Preparation Time: 20 minutes | Cooking Time: 20 minutes

Ingredients:
For Salad:
- 2 (15-ounce) cans of chickpeas, rinsed and drained
- 2½ cups cherry tomatoes, halved
- ½ bell pepper, cored and chopped
- ½ cup sun-dried tomatoes, chopped
- ½ cup olives, pitted
- 4 scallions, chopped
- ½ cup fresh mint leaves, chopped
- ½ cup fresh parsley leaves, chopped

For Dressing:
- ¼ cup olive oil
- 2 tablespoons fresh lemon juice
- 2 tablespoons white wine vinegar
- 1 garlic clove, minced
- 1 teaspoon ground sumac
- ½ teaspoon red pepper flakes, crushed
- Salt and ground black pepper, as required

Directions:
1. Add all the ingredients and mix for salad in a large bowl.
2. For the dressing, add all the ingredients in a separate bowl and whisk until well blended.
3. Place the dressing over the salad and gently toss to coat.
4. Set aside for about 30 minutes.
5. Gently stir the salad and serve.

Nutritional Information per Serving:
Calories: 216, Fat: 8.7g, Net Carbohydrates: 22.8g, Carbohydrates: 29.8g, Fiber: 7g, Sugar: 2.5g, Protein: 6.7g, Sodium: 422mg

WATERMELON SALAD

Serves: 8 individuals | Preparation Time: 15 minutes

Ingredients:
For Vinaigrette:
- 2 tablespoons fresh lime juice
- 2 tablespoons honey
- 1 tablespoon olive oil
- Pinch of salt

For Salad:
- 1 (5-pound) watermelon, peeled and cut into cubes
- 3 cups cucumber, cubed
- 4 tablespoons fresh mint leaves, torn
- ½ cup feta cheese, crumbled

Directions:
1. For the vinaigrette, add all ingredients and beat until well combined in a small bowl.
2. For the salad: in a large-sized salad bowl, mix watermelon, cucumber and mint.
3. Place the vinaigrette over the watermelon mixture and gently toss to coat.
4. Serve immediately with the garnishing of feta cheese.

Nutritional Information per Serving:
Calories: 148, Fat: 4.2g, Net Carbohydrates: 26.2g, Carbohydrates: 27.7g, Fiber: 1.5g, Sugar: 22.8g, Protein: 3.4g, Sodium: 130mg

GREENS & CARROT SALAD

Serves: 6 individuals | Preparation Time: 15 minutes | Cooking Time: 3 minutes

Ingredients:
For Salad:
- 3 tablespoons raw pine nuts
- 4 carrots, peeled and cut into thin rounds
- 4 cups fresh baby arugula
- 1 head Tuscan kale, shredded
- 1 (8-ounce) jar oil-packed sun-dried tomatoes, drained and chopped (oil reserved)
- ¼ cup fresh basil, roughly chopped
- ¼ cup fresh dill, roughly chopped
- 2 tablespoons fresh chives, chopped
- 6 ounces feta cheese, crumbled

For Vinaigrette:
- 2-3 tablespoons fresh lemon juice
- 2 tablespoons apple cider vinegar
- 1 teaspoon honey
- Pinch of red pepper flakes, crushed
- Salt and ground black pepper, as required

Directions:
1. For the salad: heat a large-sized wok over medium heat and cook the pine nuts for 2-3 minutes or until lightly golden, stirring occasionally.
2. Transfer the pine nuts onto a plate and set aside.
3. Meanwhile, in a large-sized bowl, add the carrots, arugula, kale, sun-dried tomatoes, basil, dill, and chives, and mix.
4. For the vinaigrette: in a bowl, add the reserved sun-dried tomato oil and remaining ingredients and whisk until well blended.
5. Place the vinaigrette over the salad and toss to coat well.
6. Serve immediately.

Nutritional Information per Serving:
Calories: 179, Fat: 9.3g, Net Carbohydrates: 14.6g, Carbohydrates: 17.9g, Fiber: 3.3g, Sugar: 5.7g, Protein: 8.4g, Sodium: 415mg

CHICKEN SOUP

Serves: 8 individuals | Preparation Time: 15 minutes | Cooking Time: 20 minutes

Ingredients:
- 1 tablespoon olive oil
- 1½ pounds skinless, boneless chicken breasts, cubed into ¾-inch size
- 1 tablespoon Greek seasoning
- Ground black pepper, as required
- 4 scallions, thinly sliced
- 1 garlic clove, minced
- ¼ cup white wine
- ¼ cup Greek olives, pitted and sliced
- ¼ cup sun-dried tomatoes, chopped
- 1 tablespoon capers, drained
- 1½ teaspoons fresh oregano, minced
- 1½ teaspoons fresh basil, minced
- 7 cups chicken broth
- 1½ cups uncooked orzo pasta
- 2 tablespoons fresh lemon juice
- 2 teaspoons fresh parsley, finely chopped

Directions:
1. In a large-sized Dutch oven, heat the oil over medium heat and cook the chicken breasts with Greek seasoning and black pepper for about 4-5 minutes or until golden brown from both sides.
2. With a slotted spoon, transfer the chicken breasts onto a plate and set aside.
3. In the same pan, add the scallions and garlic and sauté for about 1 minute.
4. Add the wine and remove the brown bits from the bottom of the pan.
5. Stir in the cooked chicken, olives, tomatoes, capers, oregano, basil, and broth until boiling.
6. Now, adjust the heat to low and simmer for about 15 minutes.
7. Increase the heat to medium and again bring it to a boil.
8. Stir in orzo and cook for about 8-10 minutes or until the desired doneness of the pasta.
9. Stir in the lemon juice and parsley, and serve hot.

Nutritional Information per Serving:
Calories: 298, Fat: 10.1g, Net Carbohydrates: 16.8g, Carbohydrates: 17.4g, Fiber: 0.6g, Sugar: 1.5g, Protein: 31.4g, Sodium: 875mg

MEATBALLS SOUP

Serves: 6 individuals | Preparation Time: 20 minutes | Cooking Time: 25 minutes

Ingredients:
For Meatballs:
- 1 pound lean ground turkey
- 1 garlic clove, minced
- 1 egg, beaten
- ¼ cup Parmesan cheese, grated
- Salt and ground black pepper, as required

For Soup:
- 1 tablespoon olive oil
- 1 small yellow onion, finely chopped
- 1 garlic clove, minced
- 6 cups chicken broth
- 6 cups fresh kale, trimmed and chopped
- 2 eggs, beaten lightly
- ¼ cup Parmesan cheese, grated
- Salt and ground black pepper, as required

Directions:
1. For meatballs, add all the ingredients in a bowl and mix until well combined.
2. Make small, equal-sized balls from the mixture.
3. In a large-sized soup pan, heat the oil over medium heat and sauté the onion for about 5-6 minutes.
4. Add the garlic and sauté for about 1 minute.
5. Add the broth and cook until boiling.
6. Carefully place the balls in the pan and cook until boiling.
7. Now, adjust the heat to low and simmer for about 10 minutes.
8. Stir in the kale and bring to a gentle simmer.
9. Simmer for about 2-3 minutes.
10. Slowly add the beaten eggs, stirring continuously.
11. Stir in the cheese until melted.
12. Season with salt and black pepper and serve hot.

Nutritional Information per Serving:
Calories: 317, Fat: 16.6g, Net Carbohydrates: 9.5g, Carbohydrates: 10.8g, Fiber: 1.3g, Sugar: 1.4g, Protein: 32.7g, Sodium: 800mg

LAMB SOUP

Serves: 8 individuals | Preparation Time: 15 minutes | Cooking Time: 2¼ hours

Ingredients:
- 2 pounds boneless lamb shoulder, cubed
- Salt and ground black pepper, as required
- 2 tablespoons olive oil
- 1 onion, chopped
- 2 garlic cloves, chopped
- 2 tablespoons tomato paste
- 2 teaspoons sweet paprika
- 1½ teaspoons ground cumin
- ½ teaspoon ground cloves
- 2 (14-ounce) cans of diced tomatoes with juice
- 6 cups chicken broth
- 2 (14-ounce) cans of brown lentils, drained
- 2 (14-ounce) cans of chickpeas, drained
- ½ cup fresh parsley, chopped

Directions:
1. Season the lamb cubes with salt and black pepper evenly.
2. In a large-sized saucepan, heat the oil over medium-high heat and sear the lamb cubes in 2 batches for about 4-5 minutes.
3. With a slotted spoon, transfer the lamb cubes into a bowl.
4. Add the onion and garlic over medium heat and sauté for about 3-4 minutes in the same pan.
5. Add the cooked lamb, tomato paste and spices and cook for about 1 minute.
6. Add in the tomatoes and broth and cook until boiling.
7. Now, adjust the heat to low and simmer, covered for about 1 hour.
8. Stir in the lentils and chickpeas, and simmer for about 30 minutes.
9. Uncover and simmer for about 30 minutes more.
10. Stir in the salt and black pepper and remove the soup pan from heat.
11. Serve hot with the garnishing of parsley.

Nutritional Information per Serving:
Calories: 537, Fat: 15g, Net Carbohydrates: 35.4g, Carbohydrates: 49.9g, Fiber: 14.4g, Sugar: 6.1g, Protein: 51g, Sodium: 976mg

QUINOA & LENTIL SOUP

Serves: 4 individuals | Preparation Time: 15 minutes | Cooking Time: 1 hour

Ingredients:
- ½ cup red quinoa, rinsed
- 1 cup dry lentils
- ½ cup mushrooms, sliced
- ½ cup carrots, peeled and chopped
- 1 cup celery stalk, chopped
- 1 tablespoon ground ginger
- 1 tablespoon ground cumin
- ½ tablespoon chili powder
- 1 teaspoon red pepper flakes, crushed
- 4 cups water
- 2 tablespoons fresh cilantro, chopped

Directions:
1. Mix all ingredients except cilantro over high heat in a large soup pan and cook until boiling.
2. Now, adjust the heat to medium-low and simmer, covered for about 1 hour or until the lentil becomes tender.
3. Serve hot with the garnishing of cilantro.

Nutritional Information per Serving:
Calories: 274, Fat: 2.5g, Net Carbohydrates: 27.2g, Carbohydrates: 43.7g, Fiber: 17.7g, Protein: 16.5g, Sugar: 2.3g, Sodium: 54mg

TOMATO SOUP

Serves: 8 individuals | Preparation Time: 15 minutes | Cooking Time: 8 minutes

Ingredients:
- 3 tablespoons olive oil
- 2 medium yellow onions, thinly sliced
- Salt, as required
- 3 teaspoons curry powder
- 1 teaspoon ground cumin
- 1 teaspoon ground coriander
- ½ teaspoon red pepper flakes
- 1 (15-ounce) can of diced tomatoes with juice
- 1 (28-ounce) can of plum tomatoes with juices
- 5½ cup vegetable broth
- ½ cup ricotta cheese, crumbled

Directions:
1. In a large-sized Dutch oven, heat the oil over medium-low heat and cook the onion with 1 teaspoon of salt for about 10-12 minutes, stirring occasionally.
2. Stir in the curry powder, cumin, coriander and red pepper flakes and sauté for about 1 minute.
3. Stir in the tomatoes with juices and broth and simmer for about 15 minutes.
4. Remove from heat and blend the soup until smooth with a hand blender.
5. Serve immediately with the topping of ricotta cheese.

Nutritional Information per Serving:
Calories: 135, Fat: 7.9g, Net Carbohydrates: 7.9g, Carbohydrates: 10.6g, Fiber: 2.7g, Sugar: 5.8g, Protein: 6.9g, Sodium: 573mg

CHAPTER 4:

Vegetarian Mains Recipes

CHEESY SPINACH BAKE

Serves: 5 individuals | Preparation Time: 10 minutes | Cooking Time: 38 minutes

Ingredients:
- Olive oil cooking spray
- 2 tablespoons butter, divided
- 2 tablespoons onion, chopped
- 1 pound frozen chopped spinach, thawed and squeezed
- 1½ cups heavy cream
- 3 eggs
- ½ teaspoon ground nutmeg
- Salt and ground black pepper, as required
- ½ cup Swiss cheese, shredded

Directions:
1. Preheat your oven to 375 °F.
2. Lightly grease a large-sized baking dish with cooking spray.
3. In a large-sized wok, melt 1 tablespoon of butter over medium-high heat and sauté onion for about 4-5 minutes.
4. Add in the spinach and cook for about 2-3 minutes or until all the liquid is absorbed.
5. Add cream, eggs, nutmeg, salt, and black pepper in a bowl and beat until well combined.
6. Transfer the spinach mixture to the bottom of the prepared baking dish evenly.
7. Place the egg mixture over the spinach mixture evenly and sprinkle with cheese.
8. Top with remaining butter in the shape of dots at many places.
9. Bake for approximately 25-30 minutes or until the top becomes golden brown.
10. Serve warm.

Nutritional Information per Serving:
Calories: 267, Fat: 24g, Net Carbohydrates: 3.5g, Carbohydrates: 5.6g, Fiber: 2.1g, Sugar: 1g, Protein: 9.7g, Sodium: 207mg

EGGPLANT PARMESAN

Serves: 8 individuals | Preparation Time: 20 minutes | Cooking Time: 50 minutes

Ingredients:
- Olive oil cooking spray
- 3 large eggs, beaten
- 2½ cups panko breadcrumbs
- 3 medium eggplants, cut into ¼-inch slices
- 2 (4½-ounces) jars of sliced mushrooms, drained
- ½ teaspoon dried basil
- 1/8 teaspoon dried oregano
- 2 cups mozzarella cheese, shredded
- ½ cup Parmesan cheese, shredded
- 1 (28-ounce) jar of spaghetti sauce

Directions:
1. Preheat your oven to 350 °F.
2. Generously grease a 13x9-inch baking dish with cooking spray.
3. Place eggs and breadcrumbs, respectively, in 2 different shallow bowls.
4. Dip the eggplant slices in eggs and then coat them with breadcrumbs.
5. Arrange the eggplant slices onto the prepared baking sheets in a single layer.
6. Bake for approximately 15-20 minutes or until golden brown, flipping once halfway through.
7. Again, set the temperature of the oven to 350 °F.
8. In a small-sized bowl, add mushrooms and dried herbs and mix.
9. In a separate small-sized bowl, blend both cheeses.
10. Place ½ cup of spaghetti sauce in the prepared baking dish and spread evenly.
11. Place about 1/3 of the mushroom mixture over the sauce, followed by 1/3 of the eggplant slices, ¾ cup of sauce and 1/3 of the cheese mixture.
12. Repeat the layers twice.
13. Bake for approximately 26-30 minutes or until the cheese is melted.
14. Serve warm.

Nutritional Information per Serving:
Calories: 416, Fat: 10.4g, Net Carbohydrates: 41.6g, Carbohydrates: 49.3g, Fiber: 7.7g, Sugar: 23.4g, Protein: 14.4g, Sodium: 1377mg

EGGPLANT LASAGNA

Serves: 12 individuals | Preparation Time: 20 minutes | Cooking Time: 56 minutes

Ingredients:
- 2 large eggplants, cut into 1/8-inch thick slices lengthwise
- Salt, as required
- Olive oil cooking spray
- 1 large egg
- 15 ounces of ricotta cheese
- 10 tablespoons Parmesan cheese, grated and divided
- 4 cups sugar-free tomato sauce
- 16 ounces part-skim mozzarella cheese, shredded
- 2 tablespoons fresh parsley, chopped

Directions:
1. Preheat your oven to 375 °F.
2. Arrange the eggplant slices onto a smooth surface in a single layer and sprinkle with salt.
3. Set aside for about 10 minutes.
4. With a paper towel, pat dries the eggplant slices to remove the excess moisture and salt.
5. Grease a grill pan with cooking spray and heat over medium heat.
6. Place the eggplant slices into the grill pan and cook for about 3 minutes per side.
7. Remove the eggplant slices from the grill pan and set aside.
8. In a medium-sized bowl, place the egg, ricotta cheese and ½ cup of Parmesan cheese and mix well.
9. Spread some tomato sauce evenly in the bottom of a 9x12-inch casserole dish.
10. Place 5-6 eggplant slices on top of the sauce.
11. Spread some of the cheese mixtures over eggplant slices and top with some of the mozzarella cheese.
12. Carefully repeat the layers and then sprinkle with the remaining Parmesan cheese.
13. With a lid, cover the casserole dish and bake for approximately 40 minutes.
14. Uncover the baking dish and bake for approximately 10 more minutes.
15. Remove the baking dish from the oven and set aside for about 5-10 minutes.
16. Cut into 12 equal-sized portions and serve with the garnishing of fresh parsley.

Nutritional Information per Serving:
Calories: 200, Fat: 11g, Net Carbohydrates: 6.8g, Carbohydrates: 8.4g, Fiber: 1.6g, Sugar: 4.1g, Protein: 18.2g, Sodium: 753mg

SUMMER SQUASH GRATIN

Serves: 6 individuals | Preparation Time: 15 minutes | Cooking Time: 35 minutes

Ingredients:
- 4 tablespoons olive oil, divided
- ¾ cup panko breadcrumbs
- ½ cup Parmesan cheese, grated
- 2 medium shallots, thinly sliced
- 2 garlic cloves, minced
- 2 pounds of summer squash, cut into ¼-inch pieces crosswise
- 1 tablespoon fresh thyme leaves
- 1 teaspoon lemon zest, finely grated

- Salt and ground black pepper, as required

Directions:
1. Preheat your oven to 400 °F.
2. Add 2 tablespoons of the oil, breadcrumbs and Parmesan cheese in a bowl and mix until well combined.
3. In an 8-inch cast iron wok, heat the remaining oil over medium heat and cook the shallots for about 3-4 minutes, stirring occasionally.
4. Add in the minced garlic and sauté for about 1 minute.
5. Remove the wok from heat and stir in the squash, thyme, lemon zest, salt and black pepper.
6. Then, spread the squash mixture into an even layer and sprinkle with the breadcrumbs mixture evenly.
7. Bake for approximately 25-30 minutes or until the top is golden brown.
8. Remove the wok of gratin from the oven and set aside for about 5 minutes before serving.

Nutritional Information per Serving:
Calories: 189, Fat: 12.3g, Net Carbohydrates: 7.9g, Carbohydrates: 9.7g, Fiber: 1.8g, Sugar: 5.4g, Protein: 4.8g, Sodium: 89mg

POTATO GRATIN

Serves: 6 individuals | Preparation Time: 15 minutes | Cooking Time: 55 minutes

Ingredients:
- 2 tablespoons olive oil
- 1 medium red onion, thinly sliced
- 4 garlic cloves, finely chopped
- 1½ cups milk
- 1 cup cream
- 1 teaspoon apple cider vinegar
- 4 tablespoons Parmesan cheese
- 1 fresh rosemary sprig, finely chopped
- ¼ teaspoon ground nutmeg
- Salt and ground black pepper, as required
- 2¼ pounds yellow flesh potatoes, peeled and cut into ¼-inch thick slices

Directions:
1. Preheat your oven to 390 °F.
2. In a large-sized saucepan, heat the oil over medium-high heat and sauté the onion for about 3-5 minutes.
3. Add in the garlic and sauté for about 2 minutes.
4. Add in the remaining ingredients except for potatoes and bring to a gentle simmer.
5. Cook for about 3 minutes, stirring occasionally.
6. Remove from heat and set aside.
7. Place the potato slices in the cream mixture pan and gently stir to blend.
8. Transfer the potato slices into a 9½ x9½-inch baking dish and spread in an even layer.
9. Cover the baking dish with a piece of baking paper and gently press down onto the potatoes.
10. Bake for approximately 20 minutes.
11. Remove the baking paper and bake for approximately 20 minutes.
12. Serve hot.

Nutritional Information per Serving:
Calories: 235, Fat: 9.1g, Net Carbohydrates: 29g, Carbohydrates: 33.7g, Fiber: 4.7g, Sugar: 6.3g, Protein: 6.2g, Sodium: 131mg

MUSHROOM GALETTE

Serves: 6 individuals | Preparation Time: 20 minutes | Cooking Time: 50 minutes

Ingredients:
For Crust:
- 2 cups all-purpose flour
- ½ teaspoon baking powder
- ½ teaspoon salt
- 8 tablespoons chilled butter, cut into pieces
- ½ cup water, plus more if needed

For Filling:
- 2 tablespoons butter
- 1½ pounds mixed fresh mushrooms, sliced
- ½ of onion, sliced
- 4 large garlic cloves, minced
- 2 teaspoons fresh thyme, chopped
- 1 teaspoon Italian seasoning
- Salt and ground black pepper, as required
- ¼ cup vegetable broth
- ¼ cup Parmesan cheese, shredded
- 2-3 tablespoons milk

Directions:
1. For the crust: sift together the flour, baking powder, and salt in a large-sized bowl.
2. Cut the butter into the flour with a pastry cutter until a coarse meal is formed.
3. Slowly add the water and stir until just blended.

4. With your hands, gently knead until the dough comes together.
5. Remove the dough from the bowl and transfer it onto a floured surface.
6. With your hands, flatten the dough into a disk.
7. With plastic wrap, cover the dough disk and refrigerate for at least 30 minutes.
8. Meanwhile, for filling: in a wok, melt 1 tablespoon of butter over medium heat and sauté the mushrooms for about 5 minutes.
9. Add in the remaining butter, onion, garlic, thyme, Italian seasoning, salt and black pepper and sauté for about 4-6 minutes.
10. Add the broth and cheese and cook for about 2-3 minutes, stirring frequently.
11. Remove from heat and set aside.
12. Preheat your oven to 400 °F.
13. Line a baking sheet with parchment paper.
14. Remove the plastic wrap from the dough and place it onto a lightly floured surface.
15. Roll the dough into a ¼-in thick circle with a lightly floured rolling pin.
16. Arrange the dough circle onto the prepared baking sheet.
17. Place the mushroom mixture on the dough circle, leaving about a 1-inch border.
18. Carefully fold the dough edges over the filling and then brush the edges with milk.
19. Bake for approximately 23-25 minutes or until golden brown.
20. Remove the galette from the oven and place it onto a rack to cool slightly.
21. Serve warm.

Nutritional Information per Serving:
Calories: 374, Fat: 21.3g, Net Carbohydrates: 35.4g, Carbohydrates: 38g, Fiber: 2.6g, Sugar: 2.8g, Protein: 10g, Sodium: 457mg

CABBAGE CASSEROLE

Serves: 4 individuals | Preparation Time: 15 minutes | Cooking Time: 30 minutes

Ingredients:
- ½ head cabbage
- 2 scallions, chopped
- 4 tablespoons unsalted butter
- 2 ounces cream cheese, softened
- ¼ cup Parmesan cheese, grated
- ¼ cup fresh cream
- ½ teaspoon Dijon mustard
- 2 tablespoons fresh parsley, chopped
- Salt and ground black pepper, as required

Directions:
1. Preheat your oven to 350 °F.
2. Cut the cabbage head in half, lengthwise.
3. Then cut each cabbage half into 4 equal-sized wedges.
4. Add cabbage wedges to a saucepan of boiling water and cook, covered for about 5 minutes.
5. Drain well and arrange cabbage wedges into a small-sized baking dish.
6. Melt butter and sauté onions in a small saucepan for about 5 minutes.
7. Add the remaining ingredients and stir to combine.
8. Remove from heat and immediately place the cheese mixture over cabbage wedges evenly.
9. Bake for approximately 20 minutes.
10. Remove from the oven and let it cool for about 5 minutes before serving.
11. Cut into 3 equal-sized portions and serve.

Nutritional Information per Serving:
Calories: 205, Fat: 18.6g, Net Carbohydrates: 4.2g, Carbohydrates: 6.7g, Fiber: 2.5g, Sugar: 3.4g, Protein: 4.7g, Sodium: 236mg

MUSHROOM BOURGUIGNON

Serves: 4 individuals | Preparation Time: 15 minutes | Cooking Time: 45 minutes

Ingredients:
- 1 tablespoon olive oil
- 10 ounces fresh mushrooms, sliced
- 1 small onion, chopped
- 4 garlic cloves, minced
- ¼ cup red wine
- 1 tablespoon tomato paste
- 1 teaspoon fresh thyme, chopped
- 1 teaspoon onion powder
- ¼ teaspoon red pepper flakes
- Salt, as required
- 2 cups vegetable broth
- 1 cup carrots, chopped
- 1 cup celery, chopped

- 1 tablespoon butter
- 1 tablespoon all-purpose flour
- 2 tablespoons water
- ¼ cup fresh parsley, chopped

Directions:
1. In a deep, non-stick wok, heat the oil and sauté the mushrooms, onion, and garlic for about 4-5 minutes.
2. Add the wine and cook for about 1-2 minutes, stirring frequently.
3. Add in the tomato paste, thyme, onion powder, red pepper flakes and salt and cook for about 1 minute, stirring frequently.
4. Add in the broth, carrots and celery and cook until boiling.
5. Adjust the heat to medium-low and cook, covered for about 30 minutes.
6. Meanwhile, for the flour slurry, dissolve the flour in water in a small bowl.
7. In the pan, add the flour slurry, stirring continuously.
8. Cook for about 1-2 minutes, stirring continuously.
9. Stir in the parsley and serve hot.

Nutritional Information per Serving:
Calories: 144, Fat: 7.5g, Net Carbohydrates: 9.8g, Carbohydrates: 12.5g, Fiber: 2.7g, Sugar: 4.9g, Protein: 6g, Sodium: 493mg

ZOODLES WITH MUSHROOM SAUCE

Serves: 5 individuals | Preparation Time: 20 minutes | Cooking Time: 15 minutes

Ingredients:

For Mushroom Sauce:
- 1½ tablespoons butter
- 1 large garlic clove, minced
- 1¼ cups fresh button mushrooms, sliced
- ¼ cup vegetable broth
- ¼ cup cream
- Salt and ground black pepper, as required

For Zucchini Noodles:
- 3 large zucchinis, spiralized with blade C
- ¼ cup fresh parsley leaves, chopped

Directions:
1. For the mushroom sauce: In a large-sized wok, melt the butter over medium heat and sauté the garlic for about 1 minute.
2. Stir in the mushroom slices and stir for about 6-8 minutes.
3. Stir in the broth and cook for about 2 minutes, stirring continuously.
4. Stir in the cream, salt and black pepper and cook for about 1 minute.
5. Meanwhile, for the zucchini noodles, add the zucchini noodles to a large-sized saucepan of boiling water and cook for about 2-3 minutes.
6. Transfer the zucchini noodles into a colander with a slotted spoon and immediately rinse under cold running water.
7. Drain the zucchini noodles and transfer them onto a large-sized paper towel-lined plate to drain.
8. Divide the zucchini noodles onto serving plates evenly.
9. Remove the mushroom sauce from the heat and place it over the zucchini noodles evenly.
10. Serve immediately with the garnishing of parsley.

Nutritional Information per Serving:
Calories: 77, Fat: 4.6g, Net Carbohydrates: 5.5g, Carbohydrates: 7.9g, Fiber: 2.4g, Sugar: 4g, Protein: 3.4g, Sodium: 120mg

RATATOUILLE

Serves: 4 individuals | Preparation Time: 20 minutes | Cooking Time: 45 minutes

Ingredients:
- 6 ounces tomato paste
- 3 tablespoons olive oil, divided
- ½ onion, chopped
- 3 tablespoons garlic, minced
- Salt and ground black pepper, as required
- ¾ cup water
- 1 zucchini, sliced into thin circles
- 1 yellow squash, sliced into circles thinly
- 1 eggplant, sliced into circles thinly
- 2 bell peppers (multi-colored), seeded and sliced into circles thinly
- 1 tablespoon fresh thyme leaves, minced
- 1 tablespoon fresh lemon juice

Directions:
1. Preheat your oven to 375 °F.
2. Add the tomato paste, 1 tablespoon of oil, onion, garlic, salt and black pepper in a bowl, and blend nicely.
3. Place the tomato paste mixture in the bottom of a 10x10-inch baking dish and spread evenly.

4. Arrange alternating vegetable slices, starting at the outer edge of the baking dish and working concentrically towards the center.
5. Drizzle the vegetables with the remaining oil and sprinkle with salt and black pepper, followed by the thyme.
6. Arrange a piece of parchment paper over the vegetables.
7. Bake for approximately 45 minutes.
8. Serve hot.

Nutritional Information per Serving:
Calories: 206, Fat: 11.4g, Net Carbohydrates: 18g, Carbohydrates: 26.4g, Fiber: 8.4g, Sugar: 14.1g, Protein: 5.4g, Sodium: 98mg

SQUASH & FRUIT BAKE

Serves: 4 individuals | Preparation Time: 15 minutes | Cooking Time: 40 minutes

Ingredients:
- ¼ cup water
- 1 medium butternut squash, halved and seeded
- ½ tablespoon olive oil
- ½ tablespoon balsamic vinegar
- Salt and ground black pepper, as required
- 4 large dates, pitted and chopped
- 4 fresh figs, chopped
- 3 tablespoons pistachios, chopped
- 2 tablespoons pumpkin seeds

Directions:
1. Preheat your oven to 375 ºF.
2. Place the water in the bottom of a baking dish.
3. Arrange the squash haves in a large-sized baking dish, hollow side up and drizzle with oil and vinegar.
4. Sprinkle with salt and black pepper.
5. Spread the dates, figs and pistachios on top.
6. Bake for approximately 40 minutes or until squash becomes tender.
7. Serve hot with the garnishing of pumpkin seeds.

Nutritional Information per Serving:
Calories: 227, Fat: 5.5g, Net Carbohydrates: 39.2g, Carbohydrates: 46.4g, Fiber: 7.5g, Sugar: 19.6g, Protein: 5g, Sodium: 66mg

VEGGIE COQ AU VIN

Serves: 4 individuals | Preparation Time: 15 minutes | Cooking Time: 20 minutes

Ingredients:
- 1 tablespoon olive oil
- 2 medium onions, chopped
- 3 garlic cloves, sliced
- 3 large potatoes, cut into chunky wedges
- 2 medium carrots, peeled and sliced
- 1 cup fresh mushrooms, sliced
- 2 tablespoons all-purpose flour
- 1 tablespoon tomato paste
- 9 fluid ounces of red wine
- ¾ cup vegetable broth
- 2-3 tablespoons fresh thyme, chopped

Directions:
1. Heat the olive oil in a large-sized, heavy-bottomed saucepan and sauté the onions for about 5 minutes.
2. Add in the garlic slices and sauté for about 1 minute.
3. Add in the potatoes, carrots and mushrooms and cook for about 3-4 minutes, stirring frequently.
4. Add the flour and tomato paste and stir fry for about 1-2 minutes.
5. Add the wine and simmer for about 3 minutes, stirring frequently.
6. Add the broth and thyme and simmer for about 5 minutes, stirring occasionally.
7. Serve hot with the garnishing of thyme.

Nutritional Information per Serving:
Calories: 346, Fat: 4.3g, Net Carbohydrates: 49.9g, Carbohydrates: 59.5g, Fiber: 9.6g, Sugar: 10.6g, Protein: 30.6g, Sodium: 192mg

BAKED VEGGIE STEW

Serves: 8 individuals | Preparation Time: 15 minutes | Cooking Time: 1 hour 5 minutes

Ingredients:
- 2 tablespoons olive oil
- 1 medium yellow onion, rough chopped
- 2 tablespoons garlic, minced
- 1 tablespoon all-purpose flour
- 2 tablespoons tomato paste
- ¼ cup white wine
- 1 (14½-ounce) can of petite diced tomatoes with liquid
- ½ cup vegetable broth
- ½-¾ cup water
- ¼ teaspoon baking soda
- 1½ teaspoons dried thyme, crushed
- ½ teaspoon dried oregano
- 1 teaspoon garlic powder
- 1 teaspoon onion powder
- 2 tablespoons dried onions, minced
- ½ teaspoon mustard powder
- 2 bay leaves
- Pinch of saffron threads
- Salt and ground black pepper, as required
- 2½-3 pounds of potatoes**Error! Bookmark not defined.**, scrubbed and cut into wedges
- 20 ounces fresh mushrooms, sliced
- 3 carrots, peeled and cut into chunks
- 2 celery ribs, cut into chunks
- 3 tablespoons fresh parsley, chopped

Directions:
1. Preheat your oven to 400 °F.
2. In a large-sized Dutch oven, heat the oil over medium-high heat and sauté the onion for about 4 minutes.
3. Add garlic, tomato paste, and flour, and sauté for about 1 minute.
4. Add the wine and cook for about 2-3 minutes, stirring continuously.
5. Add the tomatoes, broth, baking soda, dried herbs, spices, bay leaves and saffron and simmer for about 2 minutes, stirring continuously.
6. Remove from heat and stir in the potatoes, mushrooms, carrots and celery.
7. With a tight-fitting lid, cover the pan and immediately transfer it into the oven.
8. Bake for approximately 45 minutes.
9. Remove the pan from the oven and place over medium heat.
10. Remove the lid and cook for about 10 minutes.
11. Discard the bay leaves and serve hot with the garnishing of parsley.
12. Serve hot.

Nutritional Information per Serving:
Calories: 191, Fat: 4.2g, Net Carbohydrates: 27.5g, Carbohydrates: 33.6g, Fiber: 6.1g, Sugar: 6.8g, Protein: 6.4g, Sodium: 146mg

VEGGIE-STUFFED CABBAGE ROLLS

Serves: 4 individuals | Preparation Time: 25 minutes | Cooking Time: 40 minutes

Ingredients:
- Olive oil cooking spray

For Filling:
- 1½ cups fresh button mushrooms, chopped
- 3¼ cups zucchini, chopped
- 2 cups bell pepper (green), seeded and chopped
- ½ teaspoon dried thyme, crushed
- ½ teaspoon dried marjoram, crushed
- ½ teaspoon dried basil, crushed
- Salt and ground black pepper, as required
- ½ cup vegetable broth
- 2 teaspoons fresh lemon juice

For Rolls:
- 8 large cabbage leaves, rinsed
- 8 ounces tomato sauce
- 3 tablespoons fresh basil leaves, chopped

Directions:
1. Preheat your oven to 400 °F.
2. Lightly grease a 13x9-inch casserole dish with cooking spray.
3. For filling: in a large-sized saucepan, add all the ingredients except the lemon juice over medium heat and cook until boiling.
4. Now, adjust the heat to low and simmer, covered for about 5 minutes.
5. Remove from heat and set aside for about 5 minutes.
6. Add the lemon juice and stir to combine.
7. Meanwhile, for rolls, add the cabbage leaves to a large saucepan of boiling water and boil for about 2-4 minutes.
8. Drain the cabbage leaves well.
9. Carefully pat dry each cabbage leaf with paper towels.

10. Arrange the cabbage leaves onto a smooth surface.
11. With a knife, cut a V shape in each leaf by cutting the thick vein.
12. Carefully overlap the cut ends of each leaf.
13. Place the filling mixture over each leaf evenly and fold it on the sides.
14. Then, roll each leaf to seal the filling and secure each with toothpicks.
15. Place 1/3 cup tomato sauce in the prepared casserole dish and spread evenly.
16. Arrange the cabbage rolls over the sauce in a single layer and top with the remaining sauce evenly.
17. Cover the casserole dish and bake for approximately 15 minutes.
18. Remove from the oven and set aside, uncovered for about 5 minutes.
19. Serve warm with the garnishing of the basil.

Nutritional Information per Serving:
Calories: 67, Fat: 0.8g, Net Carbohydrates: 9.8g, Carbohydrates: 13.6g, Fiber: 3.8g, Sugar: 8.6g, Protein: 4.4g, Sodium: 450mg

4. Remove from heat and stir in the Parmesan cheese, butter, salt and black pepper
5. With a hand-held blender, blend the sauce until smooth.
6. Meanwhile, cook the gnocchi for about 3 minutes in a large saucepan of salted boiling water.
7. With a slotted spoon, transfer the gnocchi into the pan of sauce.
8. With a wooden spoon, gently mix the gnocchi with sauce and serve.

Nutritional Information per Serving:
Calories: 314, Fat: 15.2g, Net Carbohydrates: 27.2g, Carbohydrates: 30.9g, Fiber: 3.7g, Sugar: 4.1g, Protein: 7.7g, Sodium: 715mg

GNOCCHI WITH TOMATO & WINE SAUCE

Serves: 6 individuals | Preparation Time: 15 minutes | Cooking Time: 40 minutes

Ingredients:
- 2 tablespoons extra-virgin olive oil
- 6 garlic cloves
- ½ teaspoon chili flakes
- 1 cup chicken broth
- 1 cup dry white wine
- 2 (14½-ounce) cans of diced tomatoes
- ¼ cup fresh basil, chopped
- ½ cup Parmesan cheese, grated
- ¼ cup chilled butter, cut into 1-inch cubes
- Salt and ground black pepper, as required
- 1 pound gnocchi

Directions:
1. In a saucepan, add the oil, garlic and chili flakes over medium heat and cook for about 2 minutes.
2. Add the broth and wine and simmer for about 10 minutes.
3. Stir in the tomatoes and basil and simmer for about 30 minutes.

CHAPTER 5:
Fish & Seafood Recipes

SALMON WITH CAPERS

Serves: 4 individuals | Preparation Time: 10 minutes | Cooking Time: 8 minutes

Ingredients:
- 2 tablespoons olive oil
- 4 (6-ounce) salmon fillets
- 2 tablespoons capers
- Salt and ground black pepper, as required
- 4 lemon wedges

Directions:
1. In a large-sized non-stick wok, heat oil over high heat and cook the salmon fillets for about 3 minutes.
2. Sprinkle the salmon fillets with capers, salt and black pepper.
3. Flip the salmon fillets and cook for about 5 minutes or until browned.
4. Serve with the garnishing of lemon wedges.

Nutritional Information per Serving:
Calories: 286, Fat: 17.5g, Net Carbohydrates: 0.2g, Carbohydrates: 0.4g, Fiber: 0.2g, Sugar: 0.1g, Protein: 33.1g, Sodium: 241mg

SALMON WITH AVOCADO SAUCE

Serves: 4 individuals | Preparation Time: 15 minutes | Cooking Time: 8 minutes

Ingredients:
For Avocado Sauce:
- 2 avocados, peeled, pitted and chopped
- 1 cup plain Greek yogurt
- 2 garlic cloves, chopped
- 3-4 tablespoons fresh lime juice
- Salt and ground black pepper, as required

For Salmon:
- 2 teaspoons ground cumin
- 2 teaspoons garlic powder
- Salt and ground black pepper, as required
- 4 (6-ounce) skinless salmon fillets
- 2 tablespoons olive oil

Directions:
1. Add all the ingredients and pulse until smooth in a clean food processor for the avocado sauce.
2. Mix the spices, salt, and black pepper in a small bowl.
3. Coat the salmon fillets with the spice mixture evenly.
4. In a non-stick wok, heat the olive oil over medium-high heat and cook salmon fillets for about 3 minutes.
5. Flip and cook for about 4-5 minutes or until desired doneness.
6. Transfer the salmon fillets onto serving plates.

7. Top with avocado cream and serve.

Nutritional Information per Serving:
Calories: 685, Fat: 49.9g, Net Carbohydrates: 8g, Carbohydrates: 15g, Fiber: 7g, Sugar: 5.2g, Protein: 46.4g, Sodium: 293mg

SALMON IN CREAMY SAUCE

Serves: 4 individuals | Preparation Time: 15 minutes | Cooking Time: 13 minutes

Ingredients:
- ¾ teaspoon lemon pepper seasoning
- 1 teaspoon dried thyme
- 1 teaspoon dried parsley
- 4 (5-ounce) salmon fillets
- 5 tablespoons fresh lemon juice, divided
- 10 tablespoons butter, divided
- 1 shallot, minced
- 5 tablespoons white wine, divided
- 1 tablespoon white wine vinegar
- 1 cup half-and-half
- Salt and ground white pepper, as required

Directions:
1. Mix the lemon pepper seasoning and dried herbs in a small bowl.
2. In a shallow dish, place the salmon filets and rub them with 3 tablespoons of lemon juice.
3. Season the non-skin side with herb mixture. Set aside.
4. In a sauté pan, melt 2 tablespoons of butter over medium heat, and sauté the shallot for about 2 minutes.
5. Stir in the remaining lemon juice, ¼ cup of wine and vinegar and simmer for about 2-3 minutes.
6. Stir in half-and-half, salt and white pepper and cook for about 2-3 minutes.
7. Add 4 tablespoons of butter and beat until well combined.
8. Remove from heat and set aside, covered to keep warm.
9. In a wok, melt the remaining butter over medium heat.
10. Place salmon in the wok, herb side down and cook for about 1-2 minutes.
11. Transfer the salmon fillets onto a plate, herb side up.
12. In the wok, add the remaining wine, scraping up the browned bits from the bottom.
13. Place the salmon fillets into the wok, herb side up and cook for about 8 minutes.
14. Transfer the salmon fillets onto serving plates.
15. Top with pan sauce and serve.

Nutritional Information per Serving:
Calories: 610, Fat: 51g, Net Carbohydrates: 4.5g, Carbohydrates: 4.8g, Fiber: 0.3g, Sugar: 0.7g, Protein: 30.1g, Sodium: 356mg

TILAPIA PICCATA

Serves: 4 individuals | Preparation Time: 15 minutes | Cooking Time: 8 minutes

Ingredients:
- Olive oil cooking spray
- 3 tablespoons fresh lemon juice
- 2 tablespoons olive oil
- 2 garlic cloves, minced
- ½ teaspoon lemon zest, grated
- 2 teaspoons capers, drained
- 3 tablespoons fresh basil, minced and divided
- 4 (6-ounce) tilapia fillets
- Salt and ground black pepper, as required

Directions:
1. Preheat the broiler of the oven.
2. Arrange an oven rack about 4-inch from the heating element.
3. Grease a broiler pan with cooking spray.
4. In a small-sized bowl, add the lemon juice, oil, garlic and lemon zest and beat until well combined.
5. Add the capers and 2 tablespoons of basil and stir to combine.
6. Reserve 2 tablespoons of mixture in a small-sized bowl.
7. Coat the fish fillets with the remaining capers mixture and sprinkle with salt and black pepper.
8. Place the tilapia fillets onto the broiler pan and broil for about 3-4 minutes.
9. Remove from the oven and place the fish fillets onto serving plates.
10. Drizzle with reserved capers mixture and serve with the garnishing of remaining basil.

Nutritional Information per Serving:
Calories: 206, Fat: 8.7g, Net Carbohydrates: 0.7g, Carbohydrates: 0.9g, Fiber: 0.2g, Sugar: 0.3g, Protein: 31.9g, Sodium: 144mg

TILAPIA WITH RAISINS

Serves: 6 individuals | Preparation Time: 15 minutes | Cooking Time: 38 minutes

Ingredients:
- 1/3 cup olive oil
- 1 small red onion, finely chopped
- 2 large tomatoes, chopped
- 1/3 cup golden raisins
- 10 garlic cloves, chopped
- 1½ tablespoons capers
- 1½ teaspoons ground coriander
- 1 teaspoon ground cumin
- 1 teaspoon paprika
- ½ teaspoon cayenne pepper
- Salt and ground black pepper, as required
- 1½ poubds tilapia fillets
- 1 tablespoon fresh lemon juice
- 1 teaspoon lemon zest, grated
- 3 tablespoons fresh parsley, chopped

Directions:
1. Preheat your oven to 400 °F.
2. In a medium-sized, heavy-bottomed saucepan, heat the oil over medium-high heat and sauté the onion for about 3 minutes.
3. Add the tomatoes, raisins, garlic, capers, spices, a pinch of salt and black pepper and cook until boiling.
4. Now, adjust the heat to medium-low and simmer for about 15 minutes.
5. Meanwhile, rub the tilapia fillets with salt and black pepper evenly.
6. Remove the pan from heat and place about ½ of the cooked tomato sauce in the bottom of a 9½x13-inch baking dish evenly.
7. Place the fish fillets over the sauce and top with the lemon juice, lemon zest and remaining tomato sauce.
8. Bake for approximately 15-18 minutes or until the fish is done completely.
9. Serve hot with the garnishing of parsley.

Nutritional Information per Serving:
Calories: 241, Fat: 12.6g, Net Carbohydrates:1 0.5g, Carbohydrates: 12.3g, Fiber: 1.8g, Sugar: 7.1g, Protein: 22.6g, Sodium: 139mg

HALIBUT PARCEL

Serves: 4 individuals | Preparation Time: 15 minutes | Cooking Time: 40 minutes

Ingredients:
- 1 onion, chopped
- 1 large tomato, chopped
- 1 (5-ounce) jar of pitted Kalamata olives
- ¼ cup capers
- ¼ cup olive oil
- 1 tablespoon fresh lemon juice
- Salt and ground black pepper, as required
- 4 (6-ounce) halibut fillets
- 1 tablespoon Greek seasoning

Directions:
1. Preheat your oven to 350 °F.
2. Add the onion, tomato, onion, olives, capers, oil, lemon juice, salt and black pepper in a bowl, and mix well.
3. Season the halibut fillets with the Greek seasoning evenly.
4. Arrange the halibut fillets onto a large-sized piece of foil.
5. Top the fillets with the tomato mixture.
6. Carefully fold all the edges of the foil to create a packet.
7. Arrange the foil packet onto a baking sheet.
8. Bake for approximately 30-40 minutes.
9. Remove the foil packet from the oven and place it onto a platter for about 5 minutes.
10. Carefully unwrap the foil and transfer the fish mixture onto serving plates.
11. Serve hot.

Nutritional Information per Serving:
Calories: 365, Fat: 20.7g , Net Carbohydrates: 5.6g, Carbohydrates: 8.2g, Fiber: 2.6g, Sugar: 2.5g, Protein: 37.2g, Sodium: 814mg

COD WITH TOMATOES

Serves: 5 individuals | Preparation Time: 15 minutes | Cooking Time: 35 minutes

Ingredients:
- 1 teaspoon dried dill weed
- 2 teaspoons sumac
- 2 teaspoons ground coriander
- 1½ teaspoons ground cumin
- 1 teaspoon ground turmeric
- 2 tablespoons olive oil
- 1 large sweet onion, chopped
- 8 garlic cloves, chopped
- 2 jalapeño peppers, chopped
- 5 medium tomatoes, chopped
- 3 tablespoons tomato paste
- 2 tablespoons fresh lime juice
- ½ cup water
- Salt and ground black pepper, as required
- 5 (6-ounce) cod fillets

Directions:
1. For the spice mixture, add the dill weed and spices in a small bowl and mix well.
2. In a large-sized, deep wok, heat the oil over medium-high heat and sauté the onion for about 2 minutes.
3. Add the garlic and jalapeño and sauté for about 2 minutes.
4. Stir in the tomatoes, tomato paste, lime juice, water, half of the spice mixture, salt and pepper, and cook until boiling.
5. Now, adjust the heat to medium-low and cook, covered for about 10 minutes, stirring occasionally.
6. Meanwhile, season the cod fillets with the remaining spice mixture, salt and pepper evenly.
7. Place the fish fillets into the wok and gently press the tomato mixture.
8. Increase the heat to medium-high and cook for about 2 minutes.
9. Now, adjust the heat to medium and cook, covered, for about 10-15 minutes or until the desired doneness of the fish.
10. Serve hot.

Nutritional Information per Serving:
Calories: 248, Fat: 8.1g, Net Carbohydrates: 9.7g, Carbohydrates: 12.9g Fiber: 3.2g, Protein: 33.1g, Sugar: 6g, Sodium: 307mg

TUNA WITH OLIVES

Serves: 4 individuals | Preparation Time: 15 minutes | Cooking Time: 32 minutes

Ingredients:
- 6 tablespoons olive oil
- 1 large yellow onion, chopped
- 3 garlic cloves, minced and divided
- 1 cup Roma tomato, chopped
- 8 fresh basil leaves, chopped
- 4 tablespoons fresh parsley, chopped and divided
- 4 (8-ounce) tuna steaks
- Salt and ground black pepper, as required
- 1 cup black olives, pitted and sliced
- 4 teaspoons capers, rinsed

Directions:
1. In a large-sized non-stick wok, heat 3 tablespoons of olive oil over medium heat and sauté the onion for about 3 minutes.
2. Add 2 garlic cloves and sauté for about 2 minutes.
3. Stir in the tomatoes, basil and 2 tablespoons of parsley and cook for about 15 minutes, stirring occasionally.
4. Meanwhile, season the tuna steaks with salt and black pepper evenly.
5. In another large wok, heat the remaining olive oil over medium heat and sauté the remaining garlic for about 1 minute.
6. In the wok, place the tuna steaks in a single layer.
7. Increase the heat to medium-high and cook for about 2 minutes, stirring occasionally.
8. Place the tomato mixture, olives and capers over tuna steaks and gently stir to combine.
9. Now, adjust the heat to low and cook for about 5 minutes.
10. Garnish with remaining parsley and serve.

Nutritional Information per Serving:
Calories: 665, Fat: 39g, Net Carbohydrates: 5.8g, Carbohydrates: 8.5g, Fiber: 2.7g, Sugar: 2.8g, Protein: 69.3g, Sodium: 536mg

TUNA IN WINE SAUCE

Serves: 4 individuals | Preparation Time: 15 minutes | Cooking Time: 10 minutes

Ingredients:
- Olive oil cooking spray
- 4 (6-ounce) (1-inch thick) tuna steak
- 2 tablespoons olive oil, divided
- Salt and ground black pepper, as required
- 2 garlic cloves, minced
- 1 cup fresh tomatoes, chopped
- 1 cup dry white wine
- 2/3 cup olives, pitted and sliced
- ¼ cup capers, drained
- 2 tablespoons fresh thyme, chopped
- 1½ tablespoons fresh lemon zest, grated
- 2 tablespoons fresh lemon juice
- 3 tablespoons fresh parsley, chopped

Directions:
1. Preheat your grill to high heat.
2. Grease the grill grate with cooking spray.
3. Coat the tuna steaks with 1 tablespoon of olive oil and sprinkle with salt and black pepper.
4. Set aside for about 5 minutes.
5. For the sauce: in a small-sized wok, heat the remaining oil over medium heat and sauté the garlic for about 1 minute.
6. Add the tomatoes and cook for about 2 minutes.
7. Stir in the wine and cook until boiling.
8. Add the remaining ingredients except for parsley and cook, uncovered for about 5 minutes.
9. Stir in the parsley, salt and black pepper and remove from heat.
10. Meanwhile, place the tuna steaks onto the grill over direct heat and cook for about 1-2 minutes per side.
11. Serve the tuna steaks hot with the topping of sauce.

Nutritional Information per Serving:
Calories: 334, Fat: 11.2g, Net Carbohydrates: 5g, Carbohydrates: 7.3g, Fiber: 2.3g, Sugar: 2g, Protein: 41g, Sodium: 563mg

GARLICKY PRAWNS

Serves: 8 individuals | Preparation Time: 15 minutes | Cooking Time: 4 minutes

Ingredients:
- Olive oil cooking spray
- 3¼ pounds large prawns, peeled and deveined, with tails intact
- 6 large garlic cloves, minced
- 1/3 cup extra-virgin olive oil
- 2 tablespoons fresh lemon juice
- Salt and ground black pepper, as required

Directions:
1. Preheat the barbecue grill to high heat.
2. Lightly grease the grill grate with cooking spray.
3. In a bowl, add all the ingredients and toss to coat well.
4. Place the prawns onto the grill and cook for about 1-2 minutes per side.
5. Serve warm.

Nutritional Information per Serving:
Calories: 295, Fat: 11.6g, Net Carbohydrates: 3.5, Carbohydrates: 3.6g, Fiber: 0.1h, Sugar: 0.1g, Protein: 42.1g, Sodium: 470mg

SHRIMP CASSEROLE

Serves: 6 individuals | Preparation Time: 15 minutes | Cooking Time: 30 minutes

Ingredients
- ¼ cup butter
- 1 tablespoon garlic, minced

- 1½ pounds large shrimp, peeled and deveined
- ¾ teaspoon dried oregano, crushed
- ¼ teaspoon red pepper flakes, crushed
- ¼ cup fresh parsley, chopped
- ¾ cup dry vermouth
- 1 (14½-ounce) can of diced tomatoes
- 4 ounces feta cheese, crumbled

Directions:
1. Preheat your oven to 350 °F.
2. In a large-sized wok, melt butter over medium-high heat and sauté the garlic for about 1 minute.
3. Add the shrimp, oregano and red pepper flakes and cook for about 4-5 minutes.
4. Stir in the parsley and salt, immediately transfer the shrimp mixture into a casserole dish, and spread in an even layer.
5. In the same wok, add vermouth over medium heat and simmer for about 2-3 minutes or until reduced to half.
6. Stir in tomatoes and cook for about 2-3 minutes.
7. Place the tomato mixture over the shrimp mixture evenly.
8. Top with cheese evenly.
9. Bake for approximately 15-20 minutes or until the top becomes golden brown.
10. Serve hot.

Nutritional Information per Serving:
Calories: 250, Fat: 11.9g, Net Carbohydrates: 6.1g, Carbohydrates: 7.1g, Fiber: 1g, Sugar: 2.9g, Protein: 24.8g, Sodium: 414mg

MUSSELS IN WINE SAUCE

Serves: 6 individuals | Preparation Time: 15 minutes | Cooking Time: 18 minutes

Ingredients:
- 1 tablespoon olive oil
- 2 celery stalks, chopped
- 1 onion, chopped
- 4 garlic cloves, minced
- ½ teaspoon dried oregano, crushed
- 1 (15-ounce) can of diced tomatoes
- 1 teaspoon honey
- 1 teaspoon red pepper flakes, crushed
- 2 pounds mussels, cleaned
- 2 cups white wine
- Salt and ground black pepper, as required
- ¼ cup fresh basil, chopped

Directions:
1. In a large-sized wok, heat the oil over medium heat and sauté the celery, onion and garlic for about 5 minutes.
2. Add the tomato, honey and red pepper flakes and cook for about 10 minutes.
3. Meanwhile, in a large-sized saucepan, add mussels and wine and cook until boiling.
4. Simmer, covered for about 10 minutes.
5. Transfer the mussel mixture to the wok of the tomato mixture and stir to combine.
6. Add in the salt and black pepper and remove from heat.
7. Serve hot with the garnishing of basil.

Nutritional Information per Serving:
Calories: 244, Fat: 6g, Net Carbohydrates: 13.3g, Carbohydrates: 14.3g, Fiber: 1.5g, Sugar: 4.4g, Protein: 19.1g, Sodium: 473mg

OCTOPUS IN TOMATO SAUCE

Serves: 8 individuals | Preparation Time: 10 minutes | Cooking Time: 1 hour 25 minutes

Ingredients:
- 2¼ pounds fresh octopus, washed
- 1 bay leaf
- 1/3 cup water
- 4 tablespoons olive oil
- 2 onions, chopped finely
- Pinch of saffron threads, crushed
- 1 garlic clove, chopped finely
- 1 tablespoon tomato paste
- 1 (14-ounce) can of diced tomatoes
- 1 tablespoon honey
- ¾ cup red wine
- Salt and ground black pepper, as required
- ¼ cup fresh basil leaves, chopped

Directions:
1. Remove the eyes of the octopus and cut out the beak.
2. Then, clean the head thoroughly.
3. In a deep pan, add the octopus, bay leaf and water over medium heat and cook for about 20 minutes.
4. Add the wine and simmer for about 50 minutes.

5. Meanwhile, for the sauce: in a non-stick wok, heat the oil over medium heat and sauté the onions and saffron for about 3-4 minutes.
6. Add garlic and tomato paste, and sauté for about 1-2 minutes.
7. Stir in the tomatoes and honey and simmer for about 10 minutes.
8. Transfer the sauce to the pan of octopus and cooking for about 15 minutes.
9. Serve hot with the garnishing of basil

Nutritional Information per Serving:
Calories: 319, Fat: 10.1g, Net Carbohydrates: 12.5g, Carbohydrates: 13.8g, Fiber: 1.3g, Sugar: 5g, Protein: 38.4g, Sodium: 612mg

SEAFOOD BAKE

Serves: 6 individuals | Preparation Time: 15 minutes | Cooking Time: 30 minutes

Ingredients:
- Olive oil cooking spray
- 12 ounces imitation lobster meat
- 12 ounces imitation crab meat
- 6 ounces shrimp, peeled and deveined
- 1 cup mayonnaise
- 2 tablespoons scallions, sliced
- ½ cup mozzarella cheese, shredded

Directions:
1. Preheat your oven to 350 ºF.
2. Grease a baking dish with cooking spray.
3. Add the seafood, mayonnaise, and scallion in a large bowl and stir to combine.
4. Place the seafood mixture into the prepared baking dish evenly and top with Mozzarella cheese.
5. Bake for approximately 25-30 minutes.
6. Serve hot.

Nutritional Information per Serving:
Calories: 382, Fat: 29.1g, Net Carbohydrates: 1.6g, Carbohydrates: 1.7g, Fiber: 0.1g, Sugar: 0.1g, Protein: 25g, Sodium: 954mg

SEAFOOD STEW

Serves: 6 individuals | Preparation Time: 20 minutes | Cooking Time: 25 minutes

Ingredients:
- 2 tablespoons olive oil
- 1 medium onion, finely chopped
- 2 garlic cloves, minced
- ¼ teaspoon red pepper flakes, crushed
- ½ pounds plum tomatoes, seeded and chopped
- 1/3 cup white wine
- 1 cup clam juice
- 1 tablespoon tomato paste
- Salt, as required
- 1-pound snapper fillets, cubed into 1-inch size
- 1 pound large shrimp, peeled and deveined
- ½ pounds of sea scallops
- 1/3 cup fresh parsley, minced
- 1 teaspoon fresh lemon zest, finely grated

Directions:
1. In a large-sized Dutch oven, heat the oil over medium heat and sauté the onion for about 3-4 minutes.
2. Add the garlic and red pepper flakes and sauté for about 1 minute.
3. Add the tomatoes and cook for about 2 minutes.
4. Stir in the wine, clam juice, tomato paste and salt and cook until boiling.
5. Now, adjust the heat to low and simmer, covered for about 10 minutes.
6. Stir in the seafood and simmer for about 6-8 minutes.
7. Stir in the parsley and serve hot with the garnishing of lemon zest.

Nutritional Information per Serving:
Calories: 282, Fat: 6.5g, Net Carbohydrates: 10.1g, Carbohydrates: 11.4g, Fiber: 1.3g, Sugar: 3.6g, Protein: 41.2g, Sodium: 381mg

CHAPTER 6:
Poultry & Meat Recipes

CHICKEN PITA POCKETS

Serves: 4 individuals | Preparation Time: 20 minutes | Cooking Time: 8 minutes

Ingredients:

For Chicken Marinade:
- 2 tablespoons fresh lemon juice
- 3 teaspoons olive oil
- 1 tablespoon fresh oregano, chopped
- 1½ teaspoons garlic, minced
- 1 teaspoon lemon zest
- Salt ground black pepper, as required
- 1 pound chicken tenders

For Yogurt Sauce:
- 1 English cucumber, seeded and grated,
- Salt, as required
- ¾ cup plain Greek yogurt
- 2 teaspoons olive oil
- 2 teaspoons fresh dill, chopped
- 2 teaspoons fresh mint, chopped
- ½ teaspoon garlic, minced
- Ground black pepper, as required

For Pita Pockets:
- Olive oil cooking spray
- 2 (6½-inch) whole-wheat pita breads, halved
- 1 cup fresh spinach, torn
- 1 cup plum tomatoes, chopped
- ½ of English cucumber, halved and sliced
- ½ cup red onion, sliced

Directions:
1. For the marinade: Add all ingredients except chicken in a large-sized ceramic bowl and mix well.
2. Add the chicken tenders and toss to coat well in the marinade bowl.
3. Cover the bowl of chicken tenders and refrigerate to marinate for about 2 hours.
4. Meanwhile, place the cucumber in a strainer for the yogurt sauce and sprinkle with ¼ teaspoon of salt.
5. Set aside to drain for 15 minutes.
6. With your hands, squeeze the cucumber to release the liquid.
7. Transfer the cucumber to a medium-sized bowl.
8. Add the remaining sauce ingredients and stir to combine.
9. Refrigerate the sauce until ready to serve.
10. Preheat your grill to medium-high heat.
11. Lightly grease the grill grate with cooking spray.
12. Remove the chicken tenders from the bowl and shake off the excess marinade.
13. Place the chicken tenders onto the grill and cook for about 3-4 minutes per side.
14. Place some of the sauce inside each pita half evenly.
15. Fill each pita half with chicken, spinach, tomato, cumber and onion.
16. Serve with the topping of any remaining sauce.

Nutritional Information per Serving:
Calories: 427, Fat: 16.1g, Net Carbohydrates: 26.1g, Carbohydrates: 30.7g, Fiber: 4.6g, Sugar: 8.1g, Protein: 40.6g, Sodium: 357mg

BRUSCHETTA CHICKEN

Serves: 4 individuals | Preparation Time: 15 minutes | Cooking Time: 40 minutes

Ingredients:
- Olive oil cooking spray
- 4 chicken breasts
- Salt and ground black pepper, as required
- 5 small tomatoes, chopped
- 2-3 tablespoons fresh basil, chopped
- 1 garlic clove, minced
- 1 teaspoon balsamic vinegar
- 1 teaspoon olive oil

Directions:
1. Preheat your oven to 375 °F.
2. Grease a baking dish with cooking spray.
3. Rub the chicken breasts with salt and black pepper evenly.
4. Arrange the chicken breasts in the prepared baking dish in a single layer.
5. Cover the baking dish and bake for approximately 35-40 minutes or until the chicken is done completely.
6. Meanwhile, in a bowl, add the tomatoes, basil, garlic, vinegar, oil and salt mix.
7. Refrigerate until using.
8. Remove the baking dish from the oven and transfer the chicken breasts onto serving plates.
9. Top with tomato mixture and serve.

Nutritional Information per Serving:
Calories: 355, Fat: 14g, Net Carbohydrates: 3.3g, Carbohydrates: 4.7g, Fiber: 1.4g, Sugar: 3g, Protein: 50.3g, Sodium: 585mg

BRAISED CHICKEN THIGHS

Serves: 6 individuals | Preparation Time: 15 minutes | Cooking Time: 1 hour 5 minutes

Ingredients:
- 1 tablespoon white vinegar
- 1 tablespoon pomegranate molasses
- 6 large garlic cloves, chopped
- 1 tablespoon seasoning salt
- 1¼ teaspoons ground cloves
- 1½ teaspoons paprika
- 1 teaspoon ground nutmeg
- Ground black pepper, as required
- 6 chicken thighs
- 1 large red onion, sliced and divided
- 2 tablespoons extra-virgin olive oil, divided
- ½ cup dry white wine
- 2½ cup chicken broth
- 2 tablespoons pomegranate molasses
- 1 bay leaf
- 2 tablespoons dried mint leaves, crushed
- 1/3 cup pomegranate seeds

Directions:
1. Add the vinegar, molasses, garlic, and spices in a large bowl and mix well.
2. Add the chicken thighs and coat with the mixture generously.
3. In the bottom of a large-sized baking dish, spread half of the onion slices.
4. Arrange the chicken over onion slices in a single layer and refrigerate, covered for 2 hours.
5. Remove the baking dish from the oven and set aside at room temperature for about 15-20 minutes before cooking.
6. Preheat your oven to 450 °F.
7. In a large-sized heavy-bottomed wok, heat 1 tablespoon of oil over medium-high heat and cook the chicken thighs for about 2-3 minutes per side.
8. Remove from heat and place the chicken thighs in a large-sized roasting pan.
9. In the same wok, heat the remaining oil over medium-high heat and sauté the remaining onion slices for about 3-5 minutes.
10. Stir in the wine and cook for about 2-3 minutes, scraping up the browned bits from the bottom.
11. Add the pomegranate molasses, bay leaf, seasoned salt and broth and stir to combine.
12. Now, adjust the heat to medium-low and cook for about 5-7 minutes.
13. Discard the bay leaf and place the sauce over the chicken thighs in the roasting pan.
14. Cover the roasting pan and bake for approximately 20 minutes.
15. Uncover the roasting pan and arrange it on the lowest rack of the oven.
16. Bake for approximately 26-30 minutes or until chicken is cooked through.
17. Remove from oven and set aside for about 5 minutes before serving.
18. Sprinkle with dried mint and serve with the garnishing of pomegranate seeds.

Nutritional Information per Serving:
Calories: 467, Fat: 18.5g, Net Carbohydrates: 15.1g, Carbohydrates: 17.2g, Fiber: 2.1g, Sugar: 9g, Protein: 52.3g, Sodium: 1200mg

SPICED CHICKEN STEW

Serves: 4 individuals | Preparation Time: 15 minutes | Cooking Time: 52 minutes

Ingredients:
- 2 tablespoons olive oil, divided
- 4 (4-ounce) boneless, skinless chicken thighs
- 4 chicken sausage links, cut each in half
- 1 celery stalk, chopped
- 1 medium red bell pepper, seeded and chopped
- 1 tablespoon yellow onion, chopped
- 1 red hot chili pepper
- ½ cup tomato, chopped
- 1 teaspoon dried thyme
- 1 teaspoon dried oregano
- ½ teaspoon garlic powder
- 1 teaspoon smoked paprika
- 3 cups chicken broth
- 2 tablespoons fresh cilantro, chopped
- Salt and ground black pepper, as required

Directions:
1. In a large-sized saucepan, heat 1 tablespoon of oil over medium-high heat and sear the chicken thighs for about 4-5 minutes or until browned completely.
2. With a slotted spoon, transfer the chicken thighs onto a plate.
3. In the same pan, add the sausage and cook for about 4-5 minutes.
4. With a slotted spoon, place the browned sausage onto the plate with the chicken.
5. In the same pan, heat the remaining oil over medium heat and cook the bell pepper, celery, onion and red chili for about 4-5 minutes.
6. Add the tomatoes, dried herbs and spices and cook for about 1-2 minutes.
7. Stir in the cooked chicken, sausage and broth and cook until boiling.
8. Now, adjust the heat to low and simmer for about 25-30 minutes.
9. Stir in the cilantro, salt and black pepper and serve hot.

Nutritional Information per Serving:
Calories: 357, Fat: 18.6g, Net Carbohydrates: 3.8g, Carbohydrates: 5.1g, Fiber: 1.3g, Sugar: 2.9g, Protein: 41.2g, Sodium: 854mg

TURKEY BURGERS

Serves: 4 individuals | Preparation Time: 15 minutes | Cooking Time: 8 minutes

Ingredients:
For Burgers:
- Olive oil cooking spray
- 1 (2-inch) piece fresh ginger, grated
- 1 pound lean ground turkey
- 1 medium onion, grated
- 2 garlic cloves, minced
- 1 bunch of fresh mint leaves, finely chopped
- 2 teaspoons ground coriander
- 2 teaspoons ground cumin
- ½ teaspoon ground allspice
- ½ teaspoon ground cinnamon
- Salt and ground black pepper, as required
- 1 tablespoon olive oil

For Serving:
- 1 large avocado, peeled, pitted and chopped
- 6 cups fresh baby greens
- 2 tablespoons olive oil
- 1 tablespoon fresh lemon juice
- Salt and ground black pepper, as required

Directions:
1. Preheat the broiler of the oven.
2. Lightly grease a broiler pan with cooking spray.
3. For burgers, in a large-sized bowl, squeeze the juice of ginger.
4. Add remaining ingredients and mix until well combined.
5. Make equal-sized burgers from the mixture.
6. Arrange the burgers onto the prepared broiler pan and broil for about 5 minutes per side.
7. Meanwhile, for serving: in a bowl, add all ingredients and toss to coat well.
8. Divide avocado mixture and burgers onto serving plates and serve.

Nutritional Information per Serving:
Calories: 381, Fat: 28.8g, Net Carbohydrates: 4.8g, Carbohydrates: 9.8g, Fiber: 5g, Sugar: 2.1g, Protein: 24.5g, Sodium: 138mg

STUFFED LEG OF LAMB

Serves: 14 individuals | Preparation Time: 20 minutes | Cooking Time: 1¾ hours

Ingredients:
- 1/3 cup fresh parsley, minced finely
- 8 garlic cloves, minced and divided
- 3 tablespoons olive oil, divided
- Salt and ground black pepper, as required
- Olive oil cooking spray
- 1 (4-pound) boneless leg of lamb, butterflied and trimmed
- 1/3 cup yellow onion, minced
- 4 cups fresh kale, tough ribs removed and chopped
- ½ cup Kalamata olives, pitted and chopped
- ½ cup feta cheese, crumbled
- 1 teaspoon fresh lemon zest, finely grated

Directions:
1. Mix the parsley, 4 garlic cloves, 2 tablespoons of oil, salt and black pepper in a large-sized baking dish.
2. Add the leg of lamb and coat with parsley mixture generously.
3. Set aside at room temperature.
4. Preheat your oven to 450 °F.
5. Grease a shallow roasting pan with cooking spray.
6. In a large-sized wok, heat the remaining oil over medium heat and sauté the onion and remaining garlic for about 3-5 minutes.
7. Add the kale and cook for about 8-10 minutes.
8. Remove from heat and set aside to cool for at least 10 minutes.
9. Stir in the remaining ingredients.
10. Place the leg of the lamb onto a smooth surface, cut side up.
11. Place the kale mixture in the center, leaving a 1-inch border on both sides.
12. Roll the short side to seal the stuffing.
13. With a kitchen string tightly, tie the roll in many places.
14. Arrange the rolled leg of lamb into the prepared roasting pan, seam-side down.
15. Roast for approximately 15 minutes.
16. Now, adjust the temperature of the oven to 350 °F.
17. Roast for approximately 1-1¼ hours.
18. Remove the leg of lamb from the oven and set aside for about 10-20 minutes before slicing.
19. Cut the roll into desired-sized slices and serve.

Nutritional Information per Serving:
Calories: 300, Fat: 14.2g, Net Carbohydrates: 2.9g, Carbohydrates: 3.5g, Fiber: 0.6g, Sugar: 0.4g, Protein: 37.9g, Sodium: 221mg

WINE INFUSED LAMB SHANKS

Serves: 4 individuals | Preparation Time: 15 minutes | Cooking Time: 3 hours 25 minutes

Ingredients:
- 1 tablespoon olive oil
- 4 (½-pound) lamb shanks
- 2 cups green olives, pitted
- 3 carrots, peeled and cut into ½-inch pieces
- 1 large celery root, peeled and cut into ½-inch pieces
- 1 large onion, minced
- 1 garlic clove, minced
- 2 tablespoons fresh ginger, grated
- 1 cup red wine
- 4 plum tomatoes, peeled, seeded and chopped
- 2 tablespoons lemon rind, grated
- 1 bay leaf
- ¼ teaspoon ground cinnamon
- ¼ teaspoon ground coriander
- ¼ teaspoon ground cumin
- ½ teaspoon red pepper flakes, crushed
- 3 cups low-sodium chicken broth
- Salt and ground black pepper, as required
- 1 tablespoon fresh parsley leaves, minced
- 1 tablespoon fresh cilantro leaves, minced

Directions:
1. In a large-sized, heavy-bottomed pan, heat the oil over medium heat and sear the shanks for about 5 minutes per side or until golden brown.
2. With a slotted spoon, transfer the seared shanks onto a plate and set aside.
3. In the same pan, add the olives, carrots, celery, onion, garlic and ginger over medium heat and cook for about 5 minutes, stirring frequently.
4. With a slotted spoon, transfer the vegetables onto a plate and set aside.

5. In the same pan, add the wine over high heat and cook for about 5 minutes, scraping up the brown bits
6. Add the shanks, vegetables, tomatoes, lemon rind, bay leaf and spices and stir to combine.
7. Now, adjust the heat to medium-low and simmer, covered partially, for about 3 hours.
8. Add the salt and black pepper and stir to combine.
9. Serve immediately with the garnishing of parsley and cilantro.

Nutritional Information per Serving:
Calories: 554, Fat: 24.9g, Net Carbohydrates: 24.6g, Carbohydrates: 35.5g, Fiber: 10.9g, Sugar: 16.5g, Protein: 37.7g, Sodium: 900mg

PISTACHIO-TOPPED LAMB CHOPS

Serves: 4 individuals | Preparation Time: 15 minutes | Cooking Time: 8 minutes

Ingredients:
For Chops:
- ½ teaspoon ground coriander
- ½ teaspoon ground cumin
- 1/8 teaspoons ground cinnamon
- Salt and ground black pepper, as required
- 8 (4-ounce) lamb loin chops, trimmed
- 1 tablespoon olive oil

For Pistachio Topping:
- 2 tablespoons pistachios, finely chopped
- 1 garlic clove, minced
- 2 teaspoons fresh lemon peel, finely grated
- 1½ tablespoons fresh cilantro, chopped
- 1½ tablespoons fresh parsley, chopped
- Salt, as required

Directions:
1. For chops: in a large-sized bowl, mix the spices.
2. Add lamb chops and coat with spice mixture generously.
3. In a large-sized wok, heat oil over medium-high heat and sear the chops for about 4 minutes per side or until desired doneness.
4. Meanwhile, for topping: in a bowl, mix all ingredients.
5. Serve the chops with the topping of the pistachio mixture.

Nutritional Information per Serving:
Calories: 465, Fat: 21.1g, Net Carbohydrates: 0.8g, Carbohydrates: 1.2g, Fiber: 0.4g, Sugar: 0.2g, Protein: 64,2g, Sodium: 223mg

LAMB KOFTAS

Serves: 6 individuals | Preparation Time: 20 minutes | Cooking Time: 10 minutes

Ingredients:
For Koftas:
- 1 pound ground lamb
- 2 tablespoons fat-free plain Greek yogurt
- 2 tablespoons onion, grated
- 2 teaspoons garlic, minced
- 2 tablespoons fresh cilantro, minced
- 1 teaspoon ground coriander
- 1 teaspoon ground cumin
- 1 teaspoon ground turmeric
- Salt and ground black pepper, as required
- 1 tablespoon olive oil

For Serving:
- 6 tablespoons sour cream
- 6 cups lettuce, torn

Directions:
1. For koftas, add all the ingredients in a large bowl and mix until well combined.
2. Make 12 equal-sized oblong patties.
3. In a large-sized non-stick wok, heat oil over medium-high heat and cook the patties for about 10 minutes or until browned from both sides, flipping occasionally.
4. Divide the lettuce and koftas onto serving plates.
5. Top with the sour cream and serve.

Nutritional Information per Serving:
Calories: 203, Fat: 10.7g, Net Carbohydrates: 2.9g, Carbohydrates: 3.5g, Fiber: 0.6g, Sugar: 1.1g, Protein: 22.4g, Sodium: 99mg

STEAK WITH YOGURT SAUCE

Serves: 6 individuals | Preparation Time: 15 minutes | Cooking Time: 15 minutes

Ingredients:
- Olive oil cooking spray

For Steak:
- 3 garlic cloves, minced
- 2 tablespoons fresh rosemary, chopped
- Salt and ground black pepper, as required
- 2 pounds flank steak, trimmed

For Sauce:
- 1½ cups plain Greek yogurt
- 1 cucumber, peeled, seeded and finely chopped
- 1 cup fresh parsley, chopped
- 1 garlic clove, minced
- 1 teaspoon fresh lemon zest, finely grated
- 1/8 teaspoons cayenne pepper
- Salt and ground black pepper, as required

Directions:
1. Preheat your grill to medium-high heat.
2. Grease the grill grate with cooking spray.
3. For the steak: in a large-sized bowl, add all the ingredients except the steak and mix until well combined.
4. Coat the steak with the mixture generously.
5. Set aside for about 15 minutes.
6. Place the steak onto the heated grill grate and cook for about 12-15 minutes, flipping after every 3-4 minutes.
7. Remove the steak from the grill and place it on a cutting board for about 5 minutes.
8. Meanwhile, for sauce, add all the ingredients in a bowl and mix well.
9. Cut the steak into desired-sized slices and serve with the topping of yogurt sauce.

Nutritional Information per Serving:
Calories: 355, Fat: 13.7g, Net Carbohydrates: 6.8g, Carbohydrates: 8g, Fiber: 1.2g, Sugar: 5g, Protein: 46.3g, Sodium: 162mg

STUFFED STEAK

Serves: 6 individuals | Preparation Time: 15 minutes | Cooking Time: 35 minutes

Ingredients:
- 2 tablespoons dried oregano leaves
- 1/3 cup fresh lemon juice
- 2 tablespoons olive oil
- 1 (2-pound) beef flank steak, pounded into ½-inch thickness.
- 1 cup frozen chopped spinach
- 1/3 cup olive tapenade
- ¼ cup feta cheese, crumbled
- 4 cups fresh cherry tomatoes
- Salt, as required

Directions:
1. In a large-sized baking dish, add the oregano, lemon juice and oil and mix well.
2. Add the steak and coat with the marinade generously.
3. Refrigerate to marinate for about 4 hours, flipping occasionally.
4. Preheat your oven to 425 ºF.
5. Line a shallow baking dish with parchment paper.
6. Remove the steak from the baking dish, reserving the remaining marinade in a bowl.
7. Cover the bowl of marinade and refrigerate.
8. Thaw the frozen spinach and then squeeze to remove excess water. Set aside.
9. Arrange the steak onto a cutting board.
10. Place the tapenade onto the steak evenly and top with the spinach, followed by the feta cheese.
11. Carefully roll the steak tightly to form a log.
12. With 6 kitchen string pieces, tie the log at 6 places.
13. Carefully cut the log between strings into 6 equal pieces, leaving the string in place.
14. In a bowl, add the reserved marinade, tomatoes and salt and toss to coat.
15. Arrange the log pieces onto the prepared baking dish, and cut side up.
16. Now, arrange the tomatoes around the pinwheels evenly.
17. Bake for approximately 25-35 minutes.
18. Remove the baking dish of steak from the oven and set aside for about 5 minutes before serving.

Nutritional Information per Serving:
Calories: 395, Fat: 18.2g, Net Carbohydrates: 5.1g, Carbohydrates: 7.3g, Fiber: 2.2g, Sugar: 3.8g, Protein: 48.4g, Sodium: 387mg

TOMATO BRAISED BEEF

Serves: 8 individuals | Preparation Time: 15 minutes | Cooking Time: 1 hour 55 minutes

Ingredients:
- ¼ cup olive oil
- 3 pounds boneless beef chuck roast, cut into 1½-inch cubes
- 3 celery stalks, chopped
- 2 onions, chopped
- 4 garlic cloves, minced
- 2 (28-ounce) cans of Italian-style stewed tomatoes
- 1 cup dry red wine
- ½ cup fresh parsley, chopped
- 1 teaspoon dried oregano
- Salt and ground black pepper, as required

Directions:
1. In a large-sized saucepan, heat the oil over medium-high heat and sear the beef cubes for about 4-5 minutes.
2. Add the celery, onions and garlic and cook for about 5 minutes, stirring frequently.
3. Stir in the remaining ingredients and cook until boiling.
4. Now, adjust the heat to low and simmer, covered for about 1½-1¾ hours or until the desired doneness of beef.
5. Serve hot.

Nutritional Information per Serving:
Calories: 453, Fat: 17.9g, Net Carbohydrates: 8.8g, Carbohydrates: 12.1g, Fiber: 3.3g, Sugar: 6.8g, Protein: 53.9g, Sodium: 151mg

PORK CHOPS WITH MUSHROOM SAUCE

Serves: 4 individuals | Preparation Time: 15 minutes | Cooking Time: 25 minutes

Ingredients:
- 4 (½-inch thick) boneless pork chops
- ½ teaspoon paprika
- Salt and ground black pepper, as required
- 2 teaspoons olive oil
- 3 tablespoons unsalted butter, divided
- 8 ounces fresh white mushrooms, sliced
- ½ of a medium onion, finely chopped
- 2 garlic cloves, minced
- 1 tablespoon all-purpose flour
- 1½ cups chicken broth
- 1/3 cup heavy whipping cream
- 1 teaspoon hot sauce
- 1 tablespoon fresh parsley, chopped

Directions:
1. Season the pork chops with the paprika, salt and black pepper evenly.
2. In a large-sized saucepan, heat the oil and 1 tablespoon of butter over medium-high heat and sear the chops for about 3-4 minutes per side.
3. With a slotted spoon, transfer the chops onto a plate and cover them with a piece of foil to keep them warm.
4. Now melt 1 tablespoon of the remaining butter in the same saucepan over medium heat and cook the mushrooms for about 2 minutes, stirring frequently.
5. Stir in the remaining butter, onions, salt and black pepper and cook for about 3-4 minutes, stirring frequently.
6. Add in the minced garlic and cook for about 1 minute, stirring frequently.
7. Add the flour and stir vigorously for at least 30 seconds.
8. Add the broth, whipping cream, hot sauce, salt and black pepper and simmer for about 2 minutes, stirring continuously.
9. Add the pork chops and stir to combine.
10. Now, adjust the heat to low and simmer, covered for about 5-8 minutes.
11. Serve hot with the garnishing of parsley and serve.

44

Nutritional Information per Serving:
Calories: 415, Fat: 21.8g, Net Carbohydrates: 5.8g, Carbohydrates: 6.9g, Fiber: 1.1g, Sugar: 2.6g, Protein: 26.4g, Sodium: 127mg

SAUSAGE WITH BELL PEPPERS

Serves: 6 individuals | Preparation Time: 15 minutes | Cooking Time: 17 minutes

Ingredients:
- 1 tablespoon olive oil
- 8 pork sausages, sliced
- 3 large bell peppers (multi-colored), seeded and thinly sliced
- 1 teaspoon garlic powder
- Salt and ground black pepper, as required

Directions:
1. Heat the oil over medium-high heat in a large-sized wok and cook the sausage for about 8-10 minutes.
2. With a slotted spoon, transfer the sausage slices into a large-sized bowl and set aside.
3. In the same wok, add the bell peppers and garlic powder and sauté for about 3-5 minutes.
4. Stir in the sausage, salt and black pepper and cook for about 1-2 minutes.
5. Serve hot.

Nutritional Information per Serving:
Calories: 416, Fat: 33.9g, Net Carbohydrates: 3.9g, Carbohydrates: 4.8g, Fiber: 0.9g, Sugar: 3.1g, Protein: 22.2g, Sodium: 585mg

WILD BOAR STEW

Serves: 6 individuals | Preparation Time: 20 minutes | Cooking Time: 2½ hours

Ingredients:
- 1 carrot, peeled and chopped
- 1 onion, chopped
- 1 garlic clove, chopped
- 1 fresh flat-leaf parsley sprig
- 1 fresh thyme sprig
- 2 fresh sage leaves
- 2 bay leaves
- Salt, as required
- 6-8 peppercorns
- 2½ cups white wine
- 5 tablespoons white wine vinegar
- 2½ pounds lean wild boar, cubed
- 3 tablespoons extra-virgin olive oil
- 1 tablespoon butter
- 5 ounces green olives, pitted
- Ground black pepper, as required

Directions:
1. In a large-sized saucepan, add the carrot, onion, garlic, herbs, salt, peppercorns, wine and vinegar over high heat and cook until boiling.
2. Now, adjust the heat to low and simmer for about 15 minutes.
3. Remove the pan of the veggie mixture from the heat and set aside to cool completely.
4. Transfer the veggie mixture into a large-sized bowl and stir in the meat pieces.
5. Cover the bowl of the veggie mixture and refrigerate to marinate for up to 2 days, stirring occasionally.
6. Drain the meat, reserving the marinade.
7. In a large-sized Dutch oven, heat the oil and butter over medium-high heat and cook the meat for about 5-8 minutes, stirring frequently.
8. Stir half the reserved marinade, salt and black pepper and cook until boiling.
9. Now, adjust the heat to low and simmer, covered for about 1½ hours.
10. Stir in the olives and simmer for about 30 minutes.
11. Discard the herb sprigs and serve hot.

CHAPTER 7:
Rice & Grains Recipes

RICE WITH PORK

Serves: 4 individuals | Preparation Time: 15 minutes | Cooking Time: 10 minutes

Ingredients:
- ¼ cup sun-dried tomato & oregano dressing, divided
- 1 cup frozen cut green beans
- 10 ounces of chicken broth
- 1½ cups uncooked instant rice
- 1 (16-ounce) pork tenderloin, cut into 8 slices crosswise and pounded into a ½-inch thickness
- 1 teaspoon dried rosemary leaves, crushed
- 1 cup tomato, chopped
- 2 tablespoons Parmesan cheese, grated

Directions:
1. In a medium-sized saucepan, add 2 tablespoons of dressing over medium heat and cook for about 1-2 minutes or until heated through.
2. Stir in the beans and cook for about 1 minute.
3. Stir in the broth and cook until boiling.
4. Now, adjust the heat to medium-low and simmer for about 2-3 minutes.
5. Stir in the rice and cook until boiling.
6. Cover the pan of rice and remove from heat.
7. Set aside and covered for about 5 minutes or until liquid is absorbed.
8. Sprinkle the pork slices with rosemary.
9. In a large-sized non-stick wok, add the remaining dressing over medium heat and cook for about 1-2 minutes or until heated through.
10. Stir in the pork slices and cook for about 4-5 minutes per side.
11. Add the pork slices, tomato and cheese to the rice pan and stir to combine.
12. Serve hot.

Nutritional Information per Serving:
Calories: 477, Fat: 7.2g, Net Carbohydrates: 58g, Carbohydrates: 60.6g, Fiber: 2.6g, Sugar: 1.9g, Protein: 40g, Sodium: 505mg

RICE WITH BEANS

Serves: 4 individuals | Preparation Time: 15 minutes | Cooking Time: 15 minutes

Ingredients:
- 1 (15-ounce) can of cannellini beans, drained
- 1 (15-ounce) can of chickpeas, drained
- ¾ cup uncooked instant rice
- 1 (14½-ounce) can of stewed tomatoes, undrained
- 1 cup vegetable broth
- 1 teaspoon Italian seasoning
- ¼ teaspoon red pepper flakes, crushed

- 1 cup marinara sauce
- ¼ cup Parmesan cheese, grated

Directions:
1. In a large-sized wok, add all ingredients except for marinara and Parmesan and stir to combine.
2. Place the pan of beans mixture over medium-high heat and cook until boiling.
3. Now, adjust the heat to low and simmer for about 7-9 minutes or until the rice is tender.
4. Stir in the marinara sauce and cook for about 2-3 minutes or until heated, stirring occasionally.
5. Top with cheese and serve.

Nutritional Information per Serving:
Calories: 447, Fat: 5.6g, Net Carbohydrates: 67.5g, Carbohydrates: 81.3g, Fiber: 13.8g, Sugar: 10.5g, Protein: 18.6g, Sodium: 800mg

ASPARAGUS RISOTTO

Serves: 4 individuals | Preparation Time: 15 minutes | Cooking Time: 45 minutes

Ingredients:
- 15-20 fresh asparagus spears, trimmed and cut into 1½-inch pieces
- 2 tablespoons olive oil
- 1 shallot, chopped
- 1 cup onion, chopped
- 1 garlic clove, minced
- 1 cup Arborio rice, rinsed and drained
- 1 tablespoon fresh lemon zest, finely grated
- 2 tablespoons fresh lemon juice
- ½ cup dry white wine
- 5 cups hot vegetable broth
- 1 tablespoon fresh parsley, chopped
- ¼ cup Parmesan cheese, shredded
- Salt and ground black pepper, as required

Directions:
1. Add the asparagus to a large saucepan of boiling water and cook for about 2-3 minutes.
2. Drain the asparagus and rinse under cold water. Set aside.
3. In a large-sized saucepan, heat oil over medium heat and sauté the onion for about 4-5 minutes.
4. Add in the minced garlic and sauté for about 1 minute.
5. Add the rice and stir fry for about 2 minutes.
6. Add the lemon zest, juice and wine and cook for about 2-3 minutes or until all the liquid is absorbed, stirring gently.
7. Add 1 cup of broth and cook until all the broth is absorbed, stirring occasionally.
8. Repeat this process by adding ¾ cup of broth once until all the broth is absorbed. (This procedure will take about 20-30 minutes)
9. Stir in the cooked asparagus and remaining ingredients and cook for about 3-4 minutes.
10. Serve hot.

Nutritional Information per Serving:
Calories: 362, Fat: 10.6g, Net Carbohydrates: 43.7g, Carbohydrates: 47.7g, Fiber: 4g, Sugar: 4.3g, Protein: 13.7g, Sodium: 1088mg

BAKED VEGGIES RISOTTO

Serves: 6 individuals | Preparation Time: 15 minutes | Cooking Time: 20 minutes

Ingredients:
- 2 tablespoons unsalted butter
- 1 pound cremini mushrooms, cut into ¼-inch slices
- 1 garlic clove, minced
- 5 fresh thyme sprigs
- 1 pound frozen pearl
- Salt, as required
- 1½ cups Arborio
- ½ cup dry white wine
- 5 cups warm low-sodium vegetable broth
- 1 cup frozen peas
- 1 cup Parmesan cheese, grated
- Ground black pepper, as required
- 2 tablespoons fresh chives, chopped

Directions:
1. Preheat your oven to 425 °F.
2. In a large-sized Dutch oven, melt the butter over medium-high heat and sauté the mushrooms, garlic and thyme for about 5 minutes.
3. Add the onions and salt and sauté for about 2 minutes.
4. Stir in the rice and wine and cook until boiling.
5. Cook for about 1-2 minutes.
6. Now, adjust the heat to low.
7. Add 2 cups of warm broth and cook for about 5 minutes, stirring continuously.
8. Add the remaining broth and stir to combine.

9. Cover the pan and transfer into the oven.
10. Bake for approximately 15 minutes.
11. Remove from the oven and stir in the peas, cheese and black pepper.
12. Serve immediately.

Nutritional Information per Serving:
Calories: 408, Fat: 10.4g, Net Carbohydrates: 48.5g, Carbohydrates: 53.6g, Fiber: 5.1g, Sugar: 6g, Protein: 17.1g, Sodium: 544mg

RICE & SEAFOOD PAELLA

Serves: 4 individuals | Preparation Time: 20 minutes | Cooking Time: 40 minutes

Ingredients:
- 1 tablespoon extra-virgin olive oil
- 1 red bell pepper, seeded and finely chopped
- 1 large yellow onion, finely chopped
- 4 garlic cloves, minced
- 1½ cups short-grain rice
- ½ teaspoon ground turmeric
- 1 teaspoon paprika
- 1 (14-ounce) can of diced tomatoes
- 2 pinches of saffron threads, crushed
- 3 cups chicken broth
- 12 mussels, cleaned
- 12 large shrimp, peeled and deveined
- ½ cup frozen peas, thawed
- ¼ cup fresh parsley, chopped
- 1 lemon, cut into wedges

Directions:
1. In a deep, heavy-bottomed saucepan, heat the oil over medium-high heat and sauté bell pepper, onion and garlic for about 3 minutes.
2. Add the rice, turmeric and paprika and stir to combine.
3. Stir in the tomatoes, saffron and broth and cook until boiling.
4. Now, adjust the heat to low and simmer, covered for about 20 minutes.
5. Place the mussels, shrimp and peas on top and simmer, covered for about 10-15 minutes.
6. Serve hot with the garnishing of parsley and lemon wedges.

Nutritional Information per Serving:
Calories: 455, Fat: 6.8g,
Net Carbohydrates: 70.2g, Carbohydrates: 76.2g, Fiber: 6g, Sugar: 7.3g, Protein: 21g, Sodium: 775mg

CURRIED CHICKPEAS & VEGGIES

Serves: 6 individuals | Preparation Time: 20 minutes | Cooking Time: 30 minutes

Ingredients:
- 6 tablespoons olive oil, divided
- 2 carrots, peeled and chopped
- 1 sweet potato, peeled and cubed
- 1 medium eggplant, cubed
- 1 red bell pepper, seeded and chopped
- 1 green bell pepper, seeded and chopped
- 1 onion, chopped
- 3 garlic cloves, minced
- 1 tablespoon curry powder
- 1 teaspoon ground turmeric
- 1 teaspoon ground cinnamon
- Salt and ground black pepper, as required
- 1 (15-ounce) can of chickpeas, drained
- 1 zucchini, sliced
- 1 cup fresh orange juice
- ¼ cup blanched almonds
- 2 tablespoons raisins
- 10 ounces of fresh spinach

Directions:
1. In a large-sized Dutch oven, heat 3 tablespoons of oil over medium heat and sauté the carrots, sweet potato, eggplant, bell peppers and onion for about 5 minutes.
2. Meanwhile, heat the remaining oil over medium heat in another medium pan and sauté the garlic, curry powder, cinnamon, turmeric, salt and black pepper for about 3 minutes.
3. Transfer the garlic mixture to the pan of the vegetables and stir to combine.
4. Stir in the chickpeas, zucchini, orange juice, almonds, and raisins, and simmer for about 20 minutes.
5. Stir in the spinach and cook, uncovered, for about 5 minutes.
6. Serve hot.

Nutritional Information per Serving:
Calories: 323, Fat: 17.7g, Net Carbohydrates: 28g, Carbohydrates: 38g, Fiber: 10g, Sugar: 15g, Protein: 8.1g, Sodium: 259mg

BEANS & QUINOA WITH VEGGIES

Serves: 6 individuals | Preparation Time: 20 minutes | Cooking Time: 30 minutes

Ingredients:
- 2 cups water
- 1 cup dry quinoa
- 2 tablespoons coconut oil
- 1 medium onion, chopped
- 4 garlic cloves, finely chopped
- 2 tablespoons curry powder
- ½ teaspoon ground turmeric
- Cayenne pepper, as required
- Salt, as required
- 2 cups broccoli, chopped
- 1 cup fresh kale, trimmed and chopped
- 1 cup green peas, shelled
- 1 bell pepper (red, seeded and chopped
- 2 cups canned red kidney beans, drained
- 2 tablespoons fresh lime juice

Directions:
1. In a saucepan, add the water and cook until boiling over high heat.
2. Add the quinoa and stir to combine.
3. Now, adjust the heat to low and simmer for about 10-15 minutes or until all the liquid is absorbed.
4. In a large-sized cast iron wok, melt the coconut oil over medium heat and sauté the onion, garlic, curry powder, turmeric and salt for about 4-5 minutes.
5. Add the vegetables and cook for about 4-5 minutes.
6. Stir in the quinoa and beans and cook for about 2-3 minutes.
7. Drizzle with the lime juice and serve hot.

Nutritional Information per Serving:
Calories: 410, Fat: 7.5g, Net Carbohydrates: 52.8g, Carbohydrates: 67.7g, Fiber: 14.9g, Sugar: 5.1g, Protein: 21.1g, Sodium: 55mg

BEANS & TOMATO BAKE

Serves: 4 individuals | Preparation Time: 15 minutes | Cooking Time: 1 hour 10 minutes

Ingredients:
- 1 cup dried lima beans, soaked for 8 hours and drained
- 1 bay leaf
- 1 vegetable bouillon cube
- 2-3 tablespoons olive oil
- 2-3 garlic cloves, minced
- 1 small onion, finely chopped
- 1 small carrot, peeled and shredded
- 1 (15½-ounce) can of diced tomatoes
- 1 tablespoon tomato paste
- 1-2 teaspoons pure maple syrup
- 1 teaspoon red wine vinega
- 2 teaspoons dried oregano
- 1 teaspoon dried thyme
- Pinch of ground nutmeg
- Salt and ground black pepper, as required
- 3 tablespoons fresh parsley, chopped
- 3 tablespoons fresh mint, finely chopped

Directions:
1. Add the beans and bay leaf over high heat in a large-sized saucepan of water and cook until boiling.
2. Now, adjust the heat to medium and simmer for about 30 minutes.
3. Drain the beans, reserving 1 cup of the cooking liquid.
4. Dissolve the bouillon cube in the reserved hot cooking liquid.
5. Preheat your oven to 375 °F.
6. In a large-sized Dutch oven, heat the oil over medium heat and sauté the onion and garlic for about 3-4 minutes.
7. Add the carrot and cook for about 1-2 minutes.
8. Add the tomatoes, bouillon cube mixture, and ingredients except for fresh herbs and cook until boiling.
9. Adjust the heat to low and cook for about 10-12 minutes.
10. Add the beans, parsley, and mint and stir to combine.
11. Cover the pan with a piece of foil and bake for approximately 30-40 minutes.
12. Remove the foil from the Dutch oven and bake for approximately 10-15 minutes.

13. Remove the pan of beans mixture from the oven and set aside for 10 minutes before serving.

Nutritional Information per Serving:
Calories: 175, Fat: 7.5g, Net Carbohydrates: 17.7g, Carbohydrates: 32.7g, Fiber: 15g, Sugar: 6.8g, Protein: 8.9g, Sodium: 81mg

LENTIL FALAFEL BOWLS

Serves: 4 individuals | Preparation Time: 25 minutes | Cooking Time: 20 minutes

Ingredients:

For Falafel:
- 4 tablespoons fresh parsley
- 1 small red onion, roughly chopped
- 2 garlic cloves, peeled
- 1 cup red lentils, soaked overnight
- 2 tablespoons chickpea flour
- 2 tablespoons fresh lemon juice
- 2 tablespoons olive oil
- ½ teaspoon ground cumin
- Salt and ground black pepper, as required

For Eggplant:
- Olive oil cooking spray
- 1 large eggplant
- 2 tablespoons olive oil
- Salt and ground black pepper, as required

For Salad:
- 1 cup green olives, pitted
- 2 large tomatoes, sliced
- 2 cups fresh baby greens

For Dressing:
- ¼ cup tahini
- 2 garlic cloves, minced
- 2 tablespoons fresh lemon juice
- 1 tablespoon white miso
- ¼ cup water

Directions:
1. Preheat your oven to 400 °F.
2. Line a baking sheet with parchment paper.
3. For the falafel: in a food processor, add the parsley, onion and garlic and pulse until finely chopped.
4. Now, place the remaining ingredients and pulse until just combined.
5. Make small-sized patties from the mixture.
6. Arrange the patties onto the prepared baking sheet in a single layer.
7. Bake for approximately 18-20 minutes or until patties become golden brown.
8. Meanwhile, for eggplant: preheat the grill to medium-high heat.
9. Grease the grill grate with cooking spray.
10. Carefully cut the stem end off of the eggplant.
11. Then, cut the eggplant into 1-inch-thick slices lengthwise.
12. Coat the eggplant slices with oil evenly and sprinkle with salt and black pepper.
13. Place the eggplant slices onto the grill grate and cook for about 4-5 minutes per side.
14. For the dressing, add all the ingredients in a bowl and beat until well combined.
15. Divide salad ingredients and falafel patties into serving bowls evenly.
16. Drizzle with dressing and serve immediately.

Nutritional Information per Serving:
Calories: 513, Fat: 27.4g, Net Carbohydrates: 28.6g, Carbohydrates: 53g, Fiber: 24.4g, Sugar: 9.1g, Protein: 19.7g, Sodium: 529mg

CHAPTER 8:
Pasta, Couscous & Tagine Recipes

PASTA WITH VEGGIES

Serves: 6 individuals | Preparation Time: 20 minutes | Cooking Time: 12 minutes

Ingredients:
- 1 pound whole-wheat pasta
- 2 tablespoons extra-virgin olive oil
- 4 garlic cloves, sliced
- 1 cup broccoli florets
- 1 cup eggplant, chopped
- 1 bell pepper (red), seeded and chopped
- 1/3 cup sun-dried tomatoes, chopped
- 1 cup artichoke hearts, quartered
- ¼ cup Kalamata olives, pitted and sliced
- ¼ cup pine nuts
- 1 tablespoon fresh basil, minced
- 1/3 cup Parmesan cheese, grated

Directions:
1. In a large-sized saucepan of lightly salted boiling water, cook the pasta for about 8-10 minutes or according to the package's directions.
2. Drain the pasta completely and transfer it into a large-sized bowl. Set aside.
3. Meanwhile, in a large-sized heavy-bottomed wok, heat the oil over medium-high heat and sauté the garlic for about 1 minute.
4. Stir in the broccoli, eggplant, bell pepper and sun-dried tomatoes and cook for about 5-10 minutes, stirring frequently.
5. Stir in the artichokes, olives, pine nuts, and basil and cook for about 1 minute.
6. Remove the wok of veggies from the heat and immediately stir in the cooked pasta.
7. Serve with the topping of Parmesan cheese.

Nutritional Information per Serving:
Calories: 425, Fat: 15.1g, Net Carbohydrates: 50.5g, Carbohydrates: 58.7g, Fiber: 8.2g, Sugar: 8.8g, Protein: 15.8g, Sodium: 795mg

FOUR CHEESE PASTA

Serves: 8 individuals | Preparation Time: 15 minutes | Cooking Time: 45 minutes

Ingredients:
- Olive oil cooking spray
- 1 (16-ounce) package of ziti pasta
- 2 (10-ounce) cartons of refrigerated Alfredo sauce
- 1 cup sour cream
- 2 large eggs, lightly beaten
- 1 (15-ounce) carton ricotta cheese
- ½ cup Parmesan cheese, grated and divided

- ¼ cup Romano cheese, grated
- ¼ cup fresh parsley, minced
- 1¾ cups part-skim mozzarella cheese, shredded

Directions:
1. Preheat your oven to 350 °F.
2. Lightly grease a large-sized baking dish with cooking spray.
3. In a large-sized saucepan of lightly salted boiling water, cook the pasta for about 8-10 minutes or according to the package's directions.
4. Drain the pasta completely and return to the same pan.
5. Add the Alfredo sauce and sour cream to the pasta pan and stir to combine.
6. In a small-sized bowl, add the eggs, ricotta cheese, ¼ cup of Parmesan cheese, Romano cheese and parsley and mix well.
7. Place half of the pasta mixture in the prepared baking dish and top with the cheese mixture, followed by the remaining pasta mixture.
8. Sprinkle with mozzarella cheese, followed by the remaining Parmesan.
9. Cover the baking dish and bake for approximately 25 minutes.
10. Uncover the baking dish and bake for approximately 5-10 minutes or until bubbly.
11. Serve hot.

Nutritional Information per Serving:
Calories: 523, Fat: 29.5g, Net Carbohydrates: 39g, Carbohydrates: 40.1g, Fiber: 0.1g, Sugar: 2.6g, Protein: 24.2g, Sodium: 661mg

PASTA WITH BEEF

Serves: 6 individuals | Preparation Time: 20 minutes | Cooking Time: 50 minutes

Ingredients:
- 1 pound lean ground beef
- 1 tablespoon olive oil
- 1 onion, chopped
- 1 carrot, chopped
- 1 celery stalk, chopped
- 1 teaspoon garlic, minced
- 1 (32-ounce) bottle of tomato-vegetable juice cocktail
- 1 (14-ounce) can of chicken broth
- 1 tablespoon dried basil
- 1 tablespoon dried parsley
- 1 teaspoon dried oregano
- Ground black pepper, as required
- 1½ cups whole-wheat pasta
- 1 (15-ounce) can of cannellini beans, drained

Directions:
1. Heat a large-sized wok over medium-high heat and cook the beef for about 6-8 minutes, stirring occasionally.
2. Remove the wok of beef from the heat and drain the grease.
3. In a large-sized saucepan, heat oil over medium-high heat and sauté the onion, carrot and celery for about 5 minutes.
4. Add in the minced garlic and sauté for about 1 minute.
5. Stir in the juice cocktail, broth, dried herbs and black pepper and cook until boiling.
6. Now, adjust the heat to low and simmer for about 20 minutes.
7. Meanwhile, cook the pasta in a saucepan of lightly salted boiling water for about 8-10 minutes.
8. Drain the pasta.
9. Add cooked beef and beans to the soup pan and cook for about 10 minutes.
10. Divide the pasta into serving bowls.
11. Top with hot beef mixture and serve.

Nutritional Information per Serving:
Calories: 377, Fat: 9.3g, Net Carbohydrates: 32.6g, Carbohydrates: 40.5g, Fiber: 7.9g, Sugar: 10.2g, Protein: 33.3g, Sodium: 1081mg

PASTA WITH SHRIMP

Serves: 2 individuals | Preparation Time: 15 minutes | Cooking Time: 10 minutes

Ingredients:
- 4 ounces of uncooked angel hair pasta
- 2 tablespoons olive oil
- 8 jumbo shrimp, peeled and deveined
- 6 fresh asparagus spears, trimmed and cut into 2-inch pieces
- 2 garlic cloves, minced
- ½ cup fresh mushrooms, sliced
- 1 small plum tomato, peeled, seeded and chopped
- Salt, as required
- ½ cup chicken broth

- 1/8 teaspoon red pepper flakes, crushed
- 1 tablespoon fresh basil, minced
- 1 tablespoon oregano, minced
- 1 tablespoon thyme, minced
- 1 tablespoon parsley, minced
- ¼ cup Parmesan cheese, grated

Directions:
1. In a large-sized saucepan of lightly salted boiling water, cook the pasta for about 8-10 minutes or according to the package's directions.
2. Drain the pasta completely.
3. Meanwhile, in a large-sized wok, heat the oil over medium heat and cook the shrimp and asparagus for about 3-4 minutes.
4. Add in the garlic and cook for about 1 minute.
5. Add the mushrooms, tomato, pepper flakes and broth and simmer for about 2 minutes.
6. Add the pasta and herbs and toss to coat.
7. Serve hot with a sprinkling of cheese

Nutritional Information per Serving:
Calories: 466, Fat: 20.2g, Net Carbohydrates: 37.4g, Carbohydrates: 41.3g, Fiber: 3.9g, Sugar: 3.2g, Protein: 34.9g, Sodium: 591mg

COUSCOUS & VEGGIE BOWL

Serves: 6 individuals | Preparation Time: 20 minutes | Cooking Time: 5 minutes

Ingredients:
- 1½ cups vegetable broth
- 1 teaspoon ground cumin
- 1½ cups uncooked couscous
- ½ cup raisins
- 1 (16-ounce) can of chickpeas, drained
- 3 medium tomatoes, chopped
- 2 scallions, sliced
- 2 tablespoons fresh parsley, chopped
- 2 tablespoons fresh mint leaves, chopped
- 2 teaspoons fresh orange zest, grated
- 3-4 tablespoons fresh orange juice
- 1 tablespoon olive oil

Directions:
1. Add the broth and cumin over medium-high heat in a small-sized saucepan and cook until boiling.
2. Stir in couscous and immediately remove from the heat.
3. Cover the saucepan and set aside for about 5 minutes.
4. Uncover the pan and with a fork, fluff the couscous.
5. Transfer the couscous to a bowl.
6. Add the remaining ingredients and gently stir to combine.
7. Serve immediately.

Nutritional Information per Serving:
Calories: 305, Fat: 3.8g, Net Carbohydrates: 52g, Carbohydrates: 58.2g, Fiber: 6.2g, Sugar: 10.6g, Protein: 10.1g, Sodium: 262mg

COUSCOUS WITH CAULIFLOWER & DATES

Serves: 4 individuals | Preparation Time: 15 minutes | Cooking Time: 10 minutes

Ingredients:
- 2 tablespoons olive oil, divided
- 2 garlic cloves, minced
- 1¼ cups vegetable broth
- 1 cup pearl couscous
- 1 tablespoon fresh lemon juice
- 1 shallot, chopped
- 2 cups cauliflower florets
- Salt and ground black pepper, as required
- 3 tablespoons dates, pitted and chopped
- 1 teaspoon red wine vinegar
- 2 tablespoons fresh parsley, chopped

Directions:
1. For the couscous: in a large-sized saucepan, heat 1 tablespoon of oil over medium-high heat and sauté the garlic for about 1 minute.
2. Add the broth and couscous and stir to combine.
3. Now, adjust the heat to medium and simmer, covered for about 8-10 minutes or until done completely, stirring occasionally.
4. Stir in the lemon juice and remove from heat.
5. Meanwhile, in a non-stick wok, heat the remaining oil over medium heat and sauté the shallot for about 2 minutes.
6. Stir in the cauliflower and cook for about 5-6 minutes.
7. Stir in the dates and cook for about 2 minutes.
8. Stir in the vinegar, salt and black pepper and remove from heat.
9. Transfer the cauliflower mixture to the pan with couscous and stir to combine.
10. Serve warm with the garnishing of parsley.

Nutritional Information per Serving:
Calories: 275, Fat: 8g, Net Carbohydrates: 41.3g, Carbohydrates: 43.3g, Fiber: 2g, Sugar: 6.8g, Protein: 8.3g, Sodium: 295mg

COUSCOUS & VEGGIE PILAF

Serves: 4 individuals | Preparation Time: 20 minutes | Cooking Time: 22 minutes

Ingredients:
- 3 tablespoons olive oil
- 1 medium onion, chopped
- 1 medium parsnip, peeled and thinly sliced
- 1 medium carrot, peeled and thinly sliced
- 1 medium zucchini, cut into ¾-inch pieces
- 1 medium yellow squash, cut into ¾-inch pieces
- 2 garlic cloves, minced
- 1 teaspoon ground cumin
- ½ teaspoon red pepper flakes, crushed
- ½ teaspoon smoked paprika
- 1½ cups couscous
- Salt and ground black pepper, as required
- ½ cup dried apricots, chopped
- 2¼ cups vegetable broth
- ¼ cup fresh cilantro, chopped
- ½ cup almonds, toasted and chopped

Directions:
1. In a large-sized cast iron wok, heat the oil over medium-high heat and sauté the onion for about 4-5 minutes.
2. Add the parsnip and carrot and sauté for about 4-5 minutes.
3. Add the zucchini, yellow squash, garlic, and spices, and sauté for about 4-5 minutes.
4. Add in the couscous and cook for about 1½-2 minutes, stirring occasionally.
5. Stir in the apricots and broth and cook for about 5 minutes or until all the liquid is absorbed.
6. Remove the pan of pilaf from heat, and fluff the couscous completely with a fork.
7. Stir in the cilantro and almonds, and serve.

Nutritional Information per Serving:
Calories: 493, Fat: 18g, Net Carbohydrates: 60g, Carbohydrates: 68.8g, Fiber: 8.8g, Sugar: 7.7g, Protein: 16g, Sodium: 501mg

COUSCOUS STUFFED BELL PEPPERS

Serves: 4 individuals | Preparation Time: 15 minutes | Cooking Time: 40 minutes

Ingredients:
- 1 cup water
- ½ cup uncooked couscous
- Olive oil cooking spray
- 4 bell peppers, tops removed and seeded
- 2 tablespoons fresh parsley, chopped
- 1 tablespoon olive oil
- 1 tablespoon fresh lemon juice
- Salt and ground black pepper, as required

Directions:
1. Add the water over medium-high heat in a saucepan and cook until boiling.
2. Stir in the couscous and immediately cover the pan.
3. Remove the couscous pan from the heat and set aside, covered for about 10 minutes.
4. Uncover the pan and with a fork, fluff the couscous completely.
5. Set aside to cool completely.
6. Preheat your oven to 350 °F.
7. Lightly grease a medium-sized rimmed baking sheet with cooking spray.
8. Arrange the bell peppers onto the prepared baking sheet.
9. In a large-sized bowl, add the cooled couscous and remaining ingredients and mix until well combined.
10. Stuff each bell pepper with a couscous mixture.
11. Bake for approximately 35 minutes or until bell peppers is tender.

Nutritional Information per Serving:
Calories: 151, Fat: 8.8g, Net Carbohydrates: 23.2g, Carbohydrates: 26g, Fiber: 2.8g, Sugar: 6.1g, Protein: 4.1g, Sodium: 48mg

VEGGIE TAGINE

Serves: 6 individuals | Preparation Time: 15 minutes | Cooking Time: 1 hour

Ingredients:
- ¼ cup extra-virgin olive oil
- 2 medium yellow onions, chopped
- 8-10 garlic cloves, chopped
- 1 large sweet potato, peeled and cubed
- 2 large russet potatoes, peeled and cubed
- 2 large carrots, peeled and chopped
- 1 tablespoon Harissa spice blend
- 1 teaspoon ground coriander
- 1 teaspoon ground cinnamon
- ½ teaspoon ground turmeric
- Salt, as required
- 2 cups canned whole peeled tomatoes
- ½ cup dried apricots, chopped
- 4 cups vegetable broth
- 2 cups cooked chickpeas
- 2 tablespoons fresh lemon juice
- ¼ cup fresh parsley leaves, chopped

Directions:
1. In a large-sized heavy-bottomed Dutch oven, heat olive oil over medium-high heat and sauté onions for about 4-6 minutes.
2. Add in garlic and sauté for about 1 minute.
3. Add in the potatoes, carrot, spices and salt and cook for about 5-7 minutes, stirring frequently.
4. Add in the tomatoes, apricot and broth and cook for about 10 minutes.
5. Now, adjust the heat to low and simmer, covered for another 20-25 minutes or until veggies are tender.
6. Stir in chickpeas and cook for about 5 minutes.
7. Stir in lemon juice and parsley, and serve hot.

Nutritional Information per Serving:
Calories: 492, Fat: 14.2g, Net Carbohydrates: 57g, Carbohydrates: 74.6g, Fiber: 17.6g, Sugar: 15.9g, Protein: 20.2g, Sodium: 617mg

CHICKEN TAGINE

Serves: 4 individuals | Preparation Time: 15 minutes | Cooking Time: 1 hour 40 minutes

Ingredients:
For Herb Blend:
- 1½ cups water
- 2 tablespoons extra-virgin olive oil
- 2 teaspoons paprika
- 1 teaspoon ground turmeric
- 1 teaspoon ground ginger
- Salt and ground black pepper, as required
- ½ teaspoon saffron

For Tagine:
- 2 tablespoons extra-virgin olive oil
- 2 onions, chopped
- 3 garlic cloves, chopped
- 16 ounces boneless chicken breasts, cut into bite-sized pieces
- 3 large potatoes, cut into large pieces
- 2 medium carrots, cut into large pieces
- 1 cup frozen green peas
- 1 large tomato, cut into 6-8 wedges
- 3 lemon slices
- 2-3 tablespoons fresh cilantro, chopped
- 2-3 tablespoons fresh parsley, chopped

Directions:
1. Preheat your oven to 375 °F.
2. For spice blend: in a small-sized bowl, blend the water, oil, spices, salt, black pepper and saffron. Set aside.
3. In a large-sized Dutch oven, heat olive oil over medium heat and sauté onions and garlic for about 4-5 minutes.
4. Add the chicken pieces and cook for about 3-5 minutes, stirring frequently.
5. Remove the pan of mixture from heat and spread the chicken pieces in an even layer.
6. Arrange the potatoes over the chicken pieces, followed by the carrots, green peas, tomato wedges, lemon slices and fresh herbs.
7. Place the spice mixture on top evenly.
8. Cover the Dutch oven and transfer into the oven.
9. Bake for approximately 1 hour.
10. Remove the cover of the pan and bake for approximately 30 minutes more.
11. Remove the pan of tagine from heat and stir the mixture well. Serve hot.

CHAPTER 9:
Sandwiches, Pizzas & Wraps Recipes

SPINACH & TOMATO SANDWICHES

Serves: 4 individuals | Preparation Time: 15 minutes | Cooking Time: 6 minutes

Ingredients:
- 4 multi-grain sandwich thins
- 4 teaspoons olive oil
- 1 tablespoon snipped fresh rosemary
- 4 eggs
- 2 cups fresh baby spinach leaves
- 1 medium tomato, cut into 8 thin slices
- 4 tablespoons feta cheese
- 1/8 teaspoon salt
- Ground black pepper, as required

Directions:
1. Preheat your oven to 375 °F.
2. Split each sandwich thin.
3. Brush cut sides of each sandwich thin with 2 teaspoons of olive oil.
4. Arrange the sandwich thins onto a baking sheet and bake for about 5 minutes.
5. Meanwhile, in a large-sized wok, heat the remaining 2 teaspoons of olive oil with rosemary over medium-high heat.
6. Break 1 egg into the wok and cook for about 1 minute or until the whites are set.
7. With a spatula, break the egg yolk.
8. Flip the egg and cook for about 1-2 minutes or until done.
9. Transfer the egg to a plate.
10. Repeat with the remaining egg.
11. Place the bottom halves of the toasted sandwich thins onto serving plates.
12. Divide spinach among sandwich thins and top each with tomato slices, egg and 1 tablespoon of feta cheese.
13. Sprinkle each sandwich with salt and black pepper.
14. Top with the remaining sandwich thin halves and serve.

Nutritional Information per Serving:
Calories: 240, Fat: 12.3g, Net Carbohydrates: 17.9g, Carbohydrates: 24g, Fiber: 6.1g, Sugar: 2.6g, Protein: 11.6g, Sodium: 424mg

TUNA SANDWICHES

Serves: 2 individuals | Preparation Time: 10 minutes

Ingredients:
- 1 (5-ounce) can of water-packed tuna, drained
- 1 medium apple, peeled, cored and chopped
- 3 tablespoons plain Greek yogurt
- 1 teaspoon mustard
- ½ teaspoon honey
- 4 whole wheat bread slices
- 2 lettuce leaves

Directions:
1. Add the tuna, apple, yogurt, mustard, and honey in a bowl and stir to combine well.
2. Spread about ½ cup of the tuna mix over 3 bread slices.
3. Top each sandwich with 1 lettuce leaf.
4. Close with the remaining 3 bread slices.
5. Cut the sandwiches in half and serve.

Nutritional Information per Serving:
Calories: 283, Fat: 4g, Net Carbohydrates: 34g, Carbohydrates: 40.2g, Fiber: 6.2g, Sugar: 16.4g, Protein: 26.6g, Sodium: 295mg

PEAS & FETA SANDWICHES

Serves: 4 individuals | Preparation Time: 15 minutes

Ingredients:
- 1 cup boiled green peas, mashed slightly
- 1 tablespoon olive oil
- ½ cup feta cheese, crumbled
- 1 tablespoon fresh lemon juice
- 2 tablespoons fresh mint leaves, chopped
- 8 whole-wheat bread slices, toasted

Directions:
1. Mix peas, oil, feta, lemon juice, mint, salt and pepper in a bowl.
2. Spread the peas mixture over 4 bread slices evenly.
3. Cover with remaining 4 bread slices.
4. Cut the sandwiches in half and serve.

Nutritional Information per Serving:
Calories: 224, Fat: 10.1g, Net Carbohydrates: 22g, Carbohydrates: 27.3g, Fiber: 5.3g, Sugar: 4.5g, Protein: 11.2g, Sodium: 455mg

ZUCCHINI PIZZA

Serves: 5 individuals | Preparation Time: 20 minutes | Cooking Time: 35 minutes

Ingredients:
For Sauce:
- 1 tablespoon olive oil, divided
- 2 large garlic cloves, minced
- 1 (14½-ounce) can of petite diced tomatoes, drained
- ½ teaspoon Italian seasoning
- Salt and ground black pepper, as required

For Crust:
- 4 cups zucchini, grated and chopped
- Olive oil cooking spray
- 5 tablespoons almond meal
- ½ cup mozzarella cheese, finely grated
- 3 tablespoons Parmesan cheese, finely grated
- 1 egg, beaten
- 1 teaspoon dried oregano, crushed
- ½ teaspoon garlic powder
- Pinch of salt

For Topping:
- 3 ounces part-skim fresh mozzarella cheese, cut into chunks
- 10-15 large fresh basil leaves

Directions:
1. For the sauce: in a small-sized frying pan, heat ½ tablespoon of oil over medium heat and sauté the garlic for about 30 seconds.
2. Add the tomatoes and Italian seasoning and stir to combine.
3. Now, adjust the heat to very low heat and simmer until the sauce becomes thick enough.
4. Stir in the remaining oil, salt and black pepper and remove from heat.
5. Remove the pan of tomato mixture from the heat and set aside to cool.
6. Fr crust: in a microwave-safe bowl, add the zucchini and microwave on High for about 5 minutes.
7. Drain the zucchini into a colander lined with cheesecloth and keep aside to cool.
8. Preheat your oven to 450 °F.
9. Grease a large-sized baking sheet with cooking spray.
10. After cooling, squeeze the zucchini completely and transfer it into a bowl.
11. Add the almond meal, grated mozzarella, Parmesan, egg, oregano, garlic powder and salt and mix until well combined.
12. Divide the crust mixture into 2 balls and arrange them on a greased baking sheet.
13. With your fingers, press each crust ball into 2 circles. (Do not make edges too thin).
14. Arrange each crust onto a pizza stone and bake for approximately 12-13 minutes.
15. Remove the crust from the oven.
16. Spread sauce over each crust evenly and top with basil leaves and mozzarella chunks.
17. Bake for approximately 3-5 minutes.
18. Cut each pizza into desired-sized portions and serve hot.

Nutritional Information per Serving:
Calories: 263, Fat: 17.1g, Net Carbohydrates: 7.8g, Carbohydrates: 11.5g, Fiber: 3.7g, Sugar: 5.4g, Protein: 17.6g, Sodium: 370mg

FOUR-CHEESES PIZZA

Serves: 4 individuals | Preparation Time: 15 minutes | Cooking Time: 10 minutes

Ingredients:
- 1 pre-made prepared pizza crust
- 1-2 teaspoons olive oil
- 1 cup pesto sauce
- 1 cup artichoke hearts
- 1 cup sun-dried tomatoes
- 1 cup cooked spinach leaves
- ½ cup Kalamata olives
- 4 ounces feta cheese, crumbled
- 2 ounces mozzarella cheese, shredded
- 1 ounce Asiago, shredded
- 1-ounce provolone cheese, shredded

Directions:
1. Preheat your oven to 350 °F.
2. Brush the pizza crust with olive oil evenly.
3. Spread pesto over the pizza crust, leaving the edges.
4. Arrange the olives, sun-dried tomatoes, artichoke hearts, and spinach leaves over pesto and sprinkle with cheese.
5. Place the pizza directly over the oven rack and bake for approximately 10 minutes or until the cheese is melted.
6. Remove from the oven and set the pizza aside for about 5 minutes before slicing.
7. Cut into desired-sized slices and serve.

Nutritional Information per Serving:
Calories: 573, Fat: 42.7g, Net Carbohydrates: 24.9g, Carbohydrates: 28.5g, Fiber: 3.6g, Sugar: 9g, Protein: 21.7g, Sodium: 1300mg

PEPPERONI PIZZA

Serves: 6 individuals | Preparation Time: 15 minutes | Cooking Time: 20½ minutes

Ingredients:
For Crust:
- 2 cups mozzarella cheese
- 1 large egg
- 3 tablespoons cream cheese, softened
- ¾ cup almond flour
- 1 tablespoon psyllium husk
- 1 tablespoon Italian seasoning
- Salt and ground black pepper, as required
- 1 teaspoon butter, melted

For Topping:
- ½ cup tomato sauce
- 16 pepperoni slices
- 1 cup mozzarella cheese, shredded
- ¼ teaspoon dried oregano, crushed

Directions:
1. Preheat your oven to 400 °F
2. For the crust: in a microwave-safe bowl, place mozzarella cheese and microwave on High for about 90 seconds or until melted completely.
3. In the bowl of mozzarella, add eggs and cream cheese and mix until well combined.
4. In the bowl of mozzarella mixture, add the remaining ingredients and mix until the dough ball forms.
5. Coat the dough ball with melted butter and place it onto a smooth surface.
6. With your hands, press the dough ball into a circle.
7. Arrange the crust onto a baking sheet and bake for approximately 10 minutes.
8. Carefully flip the side and Bake for approximately 2-4 minutes.
9. Remove the crust from the oven.
10. Spread the tomato sauce over the crust evenly.
11. Arrange the pepperoni slices over tomato sauce evenly and sprinkle with cheese.
12. Bake for approximately 3-5 minutes.
13. Remove the pizza from the oven and sprinkle it with oregano.
14. Cut into 6 equal-sized wedges and serve.

Nutritional Information per Serving:
Calories: 253, Fat: 20.4g, Net Carbohydrates: 2.8g, Carbohydrates: 5.4g, Fiber: 2.6g, Sugar: 1.6g, Protein: 1.1g, Sodium: 494mg

CHICKPEAS WRAPS

Serves: 2 individuals | Preparation Time: 20 minutes | Cooking Time: 25 minutes

Ingredients:

For Wraps:
- 1 (15-ounce) can of chickpeas, drained, rinsed and pat dried
- 1 tablespoon olive oil
- ½ teaspoon garlic powder
- ¼ teaspoon smoked paprika
- ¼ teaspoon ground cumin
- 4 large lettuce leaves
- 1 avocado, peeled, pitted and chopped
- 1 cup cherry tomatoes, halved

For Sauce:
- ¼ cup water
- ½ cup cashews, soaked in water for 2-2½ hours and drained
- 1 teaspoon capers
- 3 tablespoons fresh lemon juice
- 1 tablespoon tahini
- 2 garlic cloves, peeled
- 2 tablespoons unsweetened almond milk
- ½ teaspoon Dijon mustard
- Salt, as required

Directions:
1. Preheat your oven to 400 °F.
2. Line a baking sheet with parchment paper.
3. Add the chickpeas, oil, spices and salt in a bowl and toss to coat well.
4. Arrange the chickpeas onto the prepared baking sheet in an even layer.
5. Bake for approximately 20-25 minutes or until crispy.
6. Meanwhile, for the sauce: in a high-power blender, add all ingredients and pulse until smooth.
7. Transfer the cashew sauce to a glass bowl and set aside.
8. Arrange the lettuce leaves onto serving plates.
9. Divide the chickpeas, avocado and tomatoes over each leaf evenly.
10. Drizzle with sauce and serve immediately.

Nutritional Information per Serving:
Calories: 163, Fat: 41.3g, Net Carbohydrates: 49.8g, Carbohydrates: 52.9g, Fiber: 13.1g, Sugar: 6.1g, Sodium: 428mg, Protein: 18.5g

VEGGIE WRAPS

Serves: 2 individuals | Preparation Time: 20 minutes | Cooking Time: 5 minutes

Ingredients:
- ½ teaspoon olive oil
- 1 red onion, thinly sliced
- ½ of small zucchini, thinly sliced
- ½ of medium bell pepper (red), seeded and thinly sliced
- 2 whole-grain tortillas, warmed
- ¼ cup hummus
- ½ cup fresh baby spinach
- 2 tablespoons feta cheese, crumbled
- 1 teaspoon dried oregano
- 1 tablespoon black olives, pitted and sliced

Directions:
1. Heat the oil over medium-low heat in a small-sized wok and sauté the onion, zucchini and bell pepper for about 5 minutes.
2. Meanwhile, in another non-stick wok, heat the tortillas until warm.
3. Place the hummus onto the center of each wrap evenly and top with spinach, followed by the sautéed vegetables, feta, oregano and olives.
4. Carefully fold the edges of each tortilla over the filling to roll it up.
5. Cut each roll in half crosswise and serve.

Nutritional Information per Serving:
Calories: 282, Fat: 10.4g, Net Carbohydrates: 30.8g, Carbohydrates: 39.2g, Fiber: 8.4g, Sugar: 6.8g, Protein: 10.4g, Sodium: 592mg

CHICKEN WRAPS

Serves: 2 individuals | Preparation Time: 15 minutes | Cooking Time: 12 minutes

Ingredients:
- 1½ tablespoons olive oil, divided
- 1 teaspoon fresh ginger, finely chopped
- 3 garlic cloves, finely chopped
- ½ pound skinless, boneless chicken breast, thinly sliced
- 2 scallions, chopped
- ½ of bell pepper (green), seeded and chopped
- ½ of carrot, peeled and chopped
- ¼ cup cabbage, chopped
- ½ teaspoon red pepper flakes, crushed
- Salt and ground black pepper, as required
- 2 pita breads
- ½ cup mayonnaise

Directions:
1. In a medium-sized, non-stick wok, heat 1 tablespoon of oil over medium heat and sauté ginger and garlic for about 30 seconds.
2. Add chicken and cook for about 5-7 minutes, stirring frequently.
3. Add scallion, bell pepper, carrot and cabbage and cook for about 2-3 minutes.
4. Stir in seasoning and remove from heat.
5. In a medium-sized non-stick frying pan, heat the remaining oil over medium heat.
6. Add pita breads, one at a time and cook for about 1 minute per side.
7. Spread the mayonnaise over each pita bread.
8. Top with chicken mixture and roll the pita bread.
9. Serve immediately.

Nutritional Information per Serving:
Calories: 662, Fat: 36.1g, Net Carbohydrates: 49.5g, Carbohydrates: 56.1g, Fiber: 6.6g, Sugar: 6.5g, Protein: 33.3g, Sodium: 893mg

CHAPTER 10:
Sauces, Dips & Dressing Recipes

BASIL PESTO SAUCE

Serves: 6 individuals | Preparation Time: 10 minutes

Ingredients:
- 2 cups fresh basil
- 4 garlic cloves, peeled
- 2/3 cup Parmesan cheese, grated
- 1/3 cup pine nuts
- ½ cup olive oil
- Salt and ground black pepper, as required

Directions:
1. Place the basil, garlic, Parmesan cheese and pine nuts in a food processor and pulse until a chunky mixture is formed.
2. Slowly add in the oil and pulse until smooth.
3. Now, add the salt and black pepper and pulse until well combined.
4. Serve immediately.

Nutritional Information per Serving:
Calories: 232, Fat: 24.2g, Net Carbohydrates: 1.4g, Carbohydrates: 1.9g, Fiber: 0.5g, Sugar: 0.3g, Protein: 5g, Sodium: 104mg

MARINARA SAUCE

Serves: 12 individuals | reparation Time: 10 minutes | Cooking Time: 10 minutes

Ingredients:
- 2 tablespoons olive oil
- 1 garlic clove, chopped
- 2 teaspoons onion flakes
- 2 teaspoons fresh thyme, finely chopped
- 2 teaspoons fresh oregano, finely chopped
- 24 ounces tomato puree
- 1 tablespoon balsamic vinegar
- 2 teaspoons sugar
- Salt and ground black pepper, as required
- 2 tablespoons fresh parsley, finely chopped

Directions:
1. In a medium-sized, non-stick saucepan, heat the olive oil over medium-low heat and sauté the garlic, onion flakes, thyme and oregano for about 3 minutes.
2. Stir in the tomato puree, vinegar, sugar, salt, and black pepper, and bring to a gentle simmer.
3. Remove from heat and stir in the parsley.
4. Set the saucepan aside at room temperature to cool completely before serving.

Nutritional Information per Serving:
Calories: 45, Fat: 8.8g, Net Carbohydrates: 4.4g, Carbohydrates: 5.9g, Fiber: 1.4g, Sugar: 4.9g, Protein: 1.1g, Sodium: 28mg

PIZZA SAUCE

Serves: 8 individuals | Preparation Time: 15 minutes | Cooking Time: 45 minutes

Ingredients:
- 2 tablespoons olive oil
- 2 anchovy fillets
- 2 tablespoons fresh oregano leaves, finely chopped
- 3 garlic cloves, minced
- ½ teaspoon dried thyme, crushed
- ½ teaspoon red pepper flakes, crushed
- 1 (28-ounces) can of whole peeled tomatoes, crushed
- ½ teaspoon sugar
- Salt, as required
- Pinch of ground black pepper
- Pinch of baking powder

Directions:
1. In a medium-sized, non-stick saucepan, heat olive oil over medium-low heat and cook the anchovy fillets for about 1 minute, stirring occasionally.
2. Add in the oregano, garlic, thyme, and red pepper flakes, and sauté for about 2-3 minutes.
3. Add in the remaining ingredients except for baking powder and bring to a gentle boil.
4. Now, adjust the heat to low and simmer for about 35-40 minutes, stirring occasionally.
5. Stir in the baking powder and remove from heat.
6. Set the saucepan aside at room temperature to cool completely before serving.

Nutritional Information per Serving:
Calories: 57, Fat: 4g, Net Carbohydrates: 3.6g, Carbohydrates: 5.3g, Fiber: 1.7g, Sugar: 2.9g, Protein: 1.4g, Sodium: 61mg

YOGURT TZATZIKI DIP

Serves: 12 individuals | Preparation Time: 10 minutes

Ingredients:
- 1 large English cucumber, peeled and grated
- Salt, as required
- 2 cups plain Greek yogurt
- 1 tablespoon fresh lemon juice
- 4 garlic cloves, minced
- 1 tablespoon fresh mint leaves, chopped
- 2 tablespoons fresh dill, chopped
- Pinch of cayenne pepper
- Ground black pepper, as required

Directions:
1. Arrange a colander in the sink.
2. Place the cucumber into the colander and sprinkle with salt.
3. Let it drain for about 10-15 minutes.
4. With your hands, squeeze the cucumber well.
5. Place the cucumber and remaining ingredients in a large-sized bowl and stir to combine.
6. Cover the bowl and refrigerate to chill for at least 4-8 hours before serving.

Nutritional Information per Serving:
Calories: 36, Fat: 0.6g, Net Carbohydrates: 4.2g, Carbohydrates: 4.5g, Fiber: 0.3g, Sugar: 3.3g, Protein: 2.7g, Sodium: 42mg

CHICKPEAS HUMMUS

Serves: 6 individuals | Preparation Time: 15 minutes

Ingredients:
- ¼ cup tahini, well-stirred

- ¼ cup fresh lemon juice
- 1 small garlic clove, minced
- 3 tablespoons extra-virgin olive oil, divided
- ½ teaspoon ground cumin
- 1 (15-ounce) can of chickpeas, drained
- 2-3 tablespoons water
- Pinch of paprika

Directions:
1. In a clean food processor, add the tahini and lemon juice and pulse for about 1 minute.
2. Add the garlic, 2 tablespoons of oil and cumin and pulse for about 30 seconds.
3. Scrape the sides and bottom of the food processor and pulse for about 30 seconds more.
4. Add half of the chickpeas and pulse for about 1 minute.
5. Add remaining chickpeas and pulse for about 1-2 minutes or until just smooth.
6. Add water and pulse until smooth.
7. Place the hummus into a serving bowl and drizzle with the remaining oil.
8. Sprinkle with paprika and serve.

Nutritional Information per Serving:
Calories: 187, Fat: 13.4g, Net Carbohydrates: 9.8g, Carbohydrates: 12.9g, Fiber: 3.1g, Sugar: 10.6g, Protein: 5g, Sodium: 132mg

EGGPLANT DIP

Serves: 6 individuals | Preparation Time: 20 minutes | Cooking Time: 40 minutes

Ingredients:
- 2 pounds Italian eggplants, halved lengthwise
- 2 medium garlic cloves, minced
- 2 tablespoons fresh lemon juice
- ¼ cup tahini
- 1/3 cup extra-virgin olive oil, plus more
- 2 tablespoons fresh parsley, chopped plus extra for garnish
- ¾ teaspoon salt
- ¼ teaspoon ground cumin
- Pinch of smoked paprika

Directions:
1. Preheat your oven to 450 °F.
2. Line a large-sized, rimmed baking sheet with parchment paper.
3. Coat the cut sides of each eggplant with a little oil.
4. Arrange the eggplant halves on the prepared baking sheet, halved sides down.
5. Roast for about 35-40 minutes or until eggplants is tender.
6. Remove the eggplant from the oven and set aside to cool for about 4-5 minutes.
7. With a large-sized spoon, scoop out the flesh, leaving the skin behind. Arrange a mesh strainer over a bowl.
8. Place the eggplant flesh into the filter and discard any stray bits.
9. With your hands, remove the moisture from the eggplant.
10. In a bowl, add the eggplant flesh, garlic and lemon juice and with a fork, mix vigorously.
11. Add the tahini and mix until well combined. Slowly add the oil, stirring continuously until creamy and smooth.
12. Add 2 tablespoons of the parsley, salt and cumin and mix well.
13. Transfer the eggplant mixture into a serving bowl and drizzle with a little oil.
14. Sprinkle with the paprika and serve with the garnishing of parsley.

Nutritional Information per Serving:
Calories: 197, Fat: 16.9g, Net Carbohydrates: 5.2g, Carbohydrates: 11.6g, Fiber: 6.4g, Protein: 3.4g, Sugar: 4.7g, Sodium: 307mg

BLUE CHEESE DRESSING

Serves: 24 individuals | Preparation Time: 10 minutes

Ingredients:
- 1 cup blue cheese, crumbled
- 1 cup sour cream
- 1 cup mayonnaise
- 2-4 drops of liquid stevia
- 2 teaspoons fresh lemon juice
- 2 teaspoons Worcestershire sauce
- 1 teaspoon hot pepper sauce
- 2 tablespoons fresh parsley, chopped
- Salt and ground black pepper, as required

Directions:
1. In a large-sized bowl, add all the ingredients and beat until well combined
2. Refrigerate to chill before serving.

CHAPTER 11:
Fruits & Sweets Recipes

POACHED PEARS

Serves: 4 individuals | Preparation Time: 15 minutes | Cooking Time: 35 minutes

Ingredients:
- 2 cups red wine
- ½ cup fresh orange juice
- ½ cup sugar
- 2 teaspoons vanilla extract
- 1 large orange peel piece
- 8-10 whole cloves
- 1 cinnamon stick
- 4 medium bosc pears, peeled

Directions:
1. In a large-sized saucepan, place all the ingredients except pears over medium heat and cook until boiling, stirring continuously.
2. Remove the pan of the wine mixture from the heat and strain the mixture.
3. Return the wine mixture to the pan alongside the orange peel piece, cloves and cinnamon over medium-low heat.
4. Place the peeled pears into the pan and simmer for about 20-25 minutes, rotating the pears after every 5 minutes.
5. Remove the saucepan from heat and let the pears cool in the poaching liquid.
6. Carefully remove the pears from the poaching liquid and place them onto a plastic wrap-lined plate.
7. Return the pan with the remaining liquid over medium-low heat and bring it to a gentle simmer.
8. Simmer for about 2-3 minutes or until the liquid thickens slightly.
9. Divide the pears onto serving plates and top each with a little syrup.

Nutritional Information per Serving:
Calories: 333, Fat: 0.4g, Net Carbohydrates: 57g, Carbohydrates: 63.6g, Fiber: 6.6g, Sugar: 49.2g, Protein: 1.1g, Sodium: 9mg

FRUITY YOGURT PARFAIT

Serves: 4 individuals | Preparation Time: 15 minutes | Cooking Time: 10 minutes

Ingredients:
- 2 cups plain Greek yogurt
- ¼ cup honey
- ¼ cup water
- 2 tablespoons sugar
- ½ teaspoon fresh lime zest, finely grated
- ¼ teaspoon ground cinnamon
- ¼ teaspoon vanilla extract
- 2 peaches, pitted and quartered
- 4 plums, pitted and quartered

- ¼ cup almonds, toasted and chopped

Directions:
1. In a medium-sized glass bowl, place the yogurt and honey and mix until well combined.
2. In a saucepan, mix the remaining ingredients except for almonds over medium heat and cook for about 8-10 minutes or until fruits become tender, stirring occasionally.
3. Remove from heat and set aside at room temperature to cool.
4. Divide half of the yogurt mixture into 4 tall serving glasses evenly.
5. Divide the fruit mixture over the yogurt evenly and top each with the remaining yogurt.
6. Garnish with almonds and serve.

Nutritional Information per Serving:
Calories: 269, Fat: 4.9g, Net Carbohydrates: 45.6g, Carbohydrates: 48.5g, Fiber: 2.9g, Sugar: 46.3g, Protein: 9.5g, Sodium: 87mg

BLUEBERRY GELATO

Serves: 6 individuals | Preparation Time: 15 minutes | Cooking Time: 10 minutes

Ingredients:
- 1½ cups fresh blueberries
- 1 tablespoon fresh lemon juice
- 2 cups unsweetened almond milk
- ¼ cup heavy cream
- ¾ cup sugar
- 4 large egg yolks
- ½ teaspoon vanilla extract
- Pinch of salt

Directions:
1. Add blueberries and lemon juice in a clean blender and pulse until smooth.
2. Through a fine sieve, strain the blueberry mixture into a bowl by pressing with the back of a wooden spoon.
3. Discard the peel and set the puree aside.
4. In a saucepan, add milk and cream over medium heat and bring to a gentle simmer.
5. Remove from heat and set aside.
6. In a bowl, add sugar and egg yolks and with an electric mixer, beat until yellow, pale and thick.
7. Add ¼ of the hot milk mixture and beat until smooth.
8. Add the mixture into the pan with the remaining milk mixture.
9. Return the pan over low heat and cook for about 4 minutes or until the mixture becomes thick, stirring continuously.
10. Remove the pan of milk mixture from the heat and immediately strain it into a bowl.
11. Immediately stir in vanilla extract, salt and strained blueberry puree.
12. Refrigerate, covered for about overnight.
13. Transfer the blueberry mixture to an ice cream maker and freeze according to the manufacturer's directions.
14. Transfer the mixture to a sealable container and freeze until set completely.

Nutritional Information per Serving:
Calories: 137, Fat: 4.6g, Net Carbohydrates: 22.8g, Carbohydrates: 23.7g, Fiber: 0.9g, Sugar: 21.6g, Protein: 1.9g, Sodium: 70mg

STRAWBERRY ZABAGLIONE

Serves: 2 individuals | Preparation Time: 10 minutes | Cooking Time: 8 minutes

Ingredients:
- ½ cup fresh strawberries, hulled and sliced
- 3 tablespoons plus 1 teaspoon white sugar, divided
- ¼ cup dry Marsala wine
- 3 large egg yolks

Directions:
1. Add the strawberries and 1 teaspoon of sugar to a bowl and gently toss to coat.
2. Cover the bowl of strawberries and set aside at room temperature for about 1 hour.
3. Now, divide the strawberry slices into 2 small serving bowls.
4. In a small-sized saucepan, add the wine, egg yolk and remaining sugar over low heat and cook for about 7-8 minutes, beating continuously.
5. Remove the pan from heat and place the custard over the strawberries.
6. Serve warm.

Nutritional Information per Serving:
Calories: 184, Fat: 6.9g, Net Carbohydrates: 21.8g, Carbohydrates: 22.5g, Fiber: 0.7g, Sugar: 20.1g, Protein: 4.3g, Sodium: 14mg

STRAWBERRY CRÈME BRÛLÉE

Serves: 9 individuals | Preparation Time: 20 minutes | Cooking Time: 1 hour 10 minutes

Ingredients:
- 2¼ cups fresh strawberries, hulled and chopped
- ½ cup granulated sugar
- 2 cups heavy cream
- 2 cups strawberry milk
- 2 teaspoons vanilla extract
- 6 egg yolks
- ½ cup powdered sugar

Directions:
1. Preheat your oven to 325 °F.
2. In a saucepan, place the strawberries and sprinkle with 1 tablespoon of sugar.
3. Place the covered pan over low heat and bring to a gentle simmer.
4. Uncover and cook for about 5-8 minutes or until a sauce-like texture is formed.
5. Remove from heat and set aside to cool slightly.
6. Add the cream and strawberry milk to the pan of strawberry sauce and beat until well combined.
7. Place the pan of sauce mixture over medium heat and cook until just scalded but not boiling.
8. Remove from heat and set aside.
9. In a large-sized bowl, add the eggs and remaining granulated Erythritol and beat until thick and pale in color.
10. Add the vanilla extract and mix well.
11. Slowly add the warmed cream mixture to the egg mixture until well blended.
12. Place the mixture into 8 shallow ramekins evenly.
13. Arrange the ramekins in a baking dish.
14. Add hot water in the baking dish, about 1-inch up sides of the ramekins.
15. Bake for approximately 45-60 minutes or until gently set in centers.
16. Remove the baking dish of ramekins from the oven and let the ramekins cool slightly.
17. Refrigerate the ramekins for at least 4 hours.
18. Just before serving, sprinkle the ramekins evenly with powdered Erythritol.
19. Holding a kitchen torch about 4-5-inch from the top, caramelize the Erythritol for about 2 minutes.
20. Set aside for 5 minutes before serving.

Nutritional Information per Serving:
Calories: 307, Fat: 16.3g, Net Carbohydrates: 36.5g, Carbohydrates: 37.2g, Fiber: 0.7g. Sugar: 33.20g, Protein: 4.9g, Sodium: 47mg

FIG CAKE

Serves: 8 individuals | Preparation Time: 15 minutes | Cooking Time: 55 minutes

Ingredients:
- Olive oil cooking spray
- 1½ cups unbleached all-purpose flour plus more for dusting
- ¾ teaspoon baking powder
- Pinch of salt
- 1 teaspoon fresh lemon zest, finely grated
- 2/3 cup white sugar
- 2 large eggs
- 1/3 cup milk
- ¼ cup olive oil
- 4 tablespoons unsalted butter, melted
- ½ teaspoon vanilla extract
- 10 ounces fresh figs, chopped

Directions:
1. Preheat your oven to 350 °F.
2. Arrange a rack in the center portion of the oven.
3. Grease a 9-inch springform pan with cooking spray and then dust it with flour lightly.
4. Sift the flour, baking powder, and salt into a large bowl.
5. Add the lemon zest and mix well.
6. In a separate bowl, add the sugar and eggs, and with a hand mixer, beat until thick and pale yellow.
7. Add the milk, oil, butter and vanilla extract and whisk until well blended.
8. Add the flour mixture and, with a wooden spoon, mix until well blended.
9. Set aside for about 10 minutes.
10. Add about ¾ of the figs to the flour mixture bowl and gently stir to combine.
11. Place the mixture into the prepared pan evenly and bake for approximately 15 minutes.
12. Remove from oven and top the cake with the remaining figs evenly.
13. Bake for approximately 35-40 minutes or until the top becomes golden brown.

14. Remove from the oven and place the pan onto a wire rack for about 10 minutes.
15. Carefully remove the cake from the pan and place it onto the wire rack to cool completely

Nutritional Information per Serving:
Calories: 365, Fat: 14.1g, Net Carbohydrates: 54g, Carbohydrates: 58.1g, Fiber: 4.1g, Sugar: 34.3g, Protein: 5.6g, Sodium: 87mg

APPLE TORTE

Serves: 8 individuals | Preparation Time: 20 minutes | Cooking Time: 1 hour 10 minutes

Ingredients:

For Crust:
- Olive oil cooking spray
- 1½ cups all-purpose flour
- ¾ cup butter, softened
- ½ cup sugar
- ½ teaspoon pure vanilla extract

For Filling:
- 2 (8-ounce) packages of cream cheese, softened
- ¼ cup granulated white sugar
- 2 large eggs
- ¾ teaspoon pure vanilla extract

For Topping:
- 3¼ cups apples, peeled, cored and sliced thinly
- ½ cup granulated white sugar
- 1 teaspoon ground cinnamon

Directions:
1. Preheat your oven to 350 ºF.
2. Grease a 10-inch Dutch oven with cooking spray.
3. For the crust: in a large-sized bowl, add all ingredients and mix until well combined.
4. In the bottom of the prepared Dutch oven, place the crust mixture and press in the bottom.
5. For the filling: in a bowl, add the cream cheese and sugar and beat until well combined.
6. In the bowl of sugar mixture, add the eggs and vanilla extract and mix well.
7. Place the filling mixture over the crust evenly and smooth the top surface with the back of a spatula.
8. Topping: Add all the ingredients to a bowl and mix well.
9. Place the apples over the cream cheese layer evenly.
10. Bake for approximately 60-70 minutes or until the center is set.

11. Remove the pan of torte from the oven and let it cool before slicing.
12. Cut into equal-sized slices and serve.

Nutritional Information per Serving:
Calories: 613, Fat: 38.4g, Net Carbohydrates: 59g, Carbohydrates: 61.9g, Fiber: 2.9g, Sugar: 41g, Protein: 8.5g, Sodium: 309mg

BLUEBERRY CLAFOUTIS

Serves: 6 individuals | Preparation Time: 15 minutes | Cooking Time: 22 minutes

Ingredients:
- 1 teaspoon coconut oil
- ½ cup whole-wheat flour
- 1/8 teaspoon ground cinnamon
- Pinch of sea salt
- 3 eggs
- ½ cup unsweetened almond milk
- 1 tablespoon coconut oil, melted
- 1 teaspoon vanilla extract
- 2 cups fresh blueberries
- ¼ cup almonds, chopped

Directions:
1. Preheat your oven to 450 ºF.
2. In a 10-inch Dutch oven, add 1 teaspoon of coconut oil and place into the oven to preheat.
3. Add the flour, cinnamon, and salt in a large bowl and mix well.
4. In a separate bowl, add eggs, almond milk, melted coconut oil and vanilla extract and beat until well combined.
5. Add the egg mixture into the bowl of the flour mixture and mix until well combined.
6. Remove the Dutch oven and tilt it to spread the melted butter evenly.
7. Place blueberries in the bottom of the pan in a single layer.
8. Place the flour mixture over the blueberries evenly and top with almonds.
9. Bake for approximately 16-20 minutes or until a wooden skewer inserted in the center comes out clean.
10. Remove from the Dutch oven and let it cool completely before slicing.
11. Cut into equal-sized wedges and serve.

90 DAYS MEAL PLAN

	BREAKFAST	LUNCH	DINNER
DAY 1	Multi-Grain Bread	Eggplant Parmesan	Salmon with Capers
DAY 2	Yogurt Oatmeal	Chicken Pita Pockets	Pasta with Shrimp
DAY 3	Mixed Veggie Muffins	Tomato Soup	Chicken Tagine
DAY 4	Yogurt Waffles	Lamb Koftas	Curried Chickpeas & Veggies
DAY 5	Potato Omelet	Lentil Falafel Bowl	Spiced Chicken Stew
DAY 6	Yogurt with Caramelized Figs	Couscous Stuffed Bell Peppers	Sausage with Bell Peppers
DAY 7	Ricotta Pancakes	Asparagus Risotto	Stuffed Steak
DAY 8	Ham Quiche	Greens & Carrot Salad	Stuffed Leg of Lamb
DAY 9	Avocado & Eggs Toast	Four Cheese Pasta	Tomato Braised Beef
DAY 10	Ricotta Pancakes	Tuna Sandwiches	Lentil & Quinoa Casserole
DAY 11	Shakshuka	Pepperoni Pizza	Chicken Salad
DAY 12	Yogurt Oatmeal	Zoodles with Mushroom Sauce	Shrimp Casserole
DAY 13	Ham Quiche	Chickpeas Wraps	Chicken Soup
DAY 14	Potato Omelet	Zucchini Pizza	Pork Chops with Mushroom Sauce
DAY 15	Yogurt Waffles	Turkey Burgers	Baked Veggie Stew
DAY 16	Mixed Veggie Muffins	Couscous with Cauliflower & Dates	Tilapia Piccata
DAY 17	Yogurt with Caramelized Figs	Chicken Wraps	Rice with Pork
DAY 18	Ricotta Pancakes	Lamb Koftas	Quinoa & Lentil Soup
DAY 19	Multi-Grain Bread	Peas & Feta Sandwiches	Rice & Seafood Paella
DAY 20	Potato Omelet	Asparagus Risotto	Wine Infused Lamb Shanks
DAY 21	Ham Quiche	Four Cheese Pasta	Braised Chicken Thighs
DAY 22	Shakshuka	Watermelon Salad	Steak with Yogurt Sauce
DAY 23	Yogurt Oatmeal	Veggie Wraps	Tuna in Wine Sauce
DAY 24	Mixed Veggie Muffins	Garlicky Prawns	Meatballs Soup
DAY 25	Yogurt Waffles	Veggie-Stuffed Cabbage Rolls	Wild Boar Stew
DAY 26	Multi-Grain Bread	Couscous & Veggie Bowl	Bruschetta Chicken
DAY 27	Yogurt with Caramelized Figs	Turkey Burgers	Beans & Quinoa with Veggies
DAY 28	Avocado & Eggs Toast	Gnocchi with Tomato & Wine Sauce	Seafood Bake
DAY 29	Ham Quiche	Toasted Ravioli	Cod with Tomatoes
DAY 30	Bruschetta Chicken	Chickpeas Wrap	Pork Chops with Mushroom Sauce

	BREAKFAST	LUNCH	DINNER
DAY 31	Shakshuka	Chicken Salad	Salmon in Creamy Sauce
DAY 32	Cucumber and Walnut Platter	Eggplant Lasagna	Lamb Koftas
DAY 33	Potato Omelet	Shrimp Casserole	Chicken Pita Pockets
DAY 34	Deli Meat Antipasti	Lentil & Quinoa Casserole	Four Cheese Pasta
DAY 35	Ricotta Pancakes	Lentil Falafel Bowls	Rice with Pork
DAY 36	Stuffed Mushroom	Toasted Ravioli	Pasta with Veggies
DAY 37	Avocado & Eggs Toast	Spinach & Tomato Sandwich	Asparagus Risotto
DAY 38	Tuna Croquettes	Eggplant Parmesan	Tomato Braised Beef
DAY 39	Apple Torte	Tuna Sandwich	Stuffed Steak
DAY 40	Blueberry Clafoutis	Pasta with Beef	Wine-Infused Lamb Shank
DAY 41	Yogurt Waffles	Veggie Stuffed Cabbage Rolls	Spiced Chicken Stew
DAY 42	Ham Quiche	Rice with Beans	Rice & Seafood Paella
DAY 43	Ratatouille	Baked Veggies Risotto	Octopus in Tomato Sauce
DAY 44	Stuffed Mushroom	Gnocchi with Tomato & Wine Sauce	Salmon with Capers
DAY 45	Mixed Veggie Muffins	Chicken Tagine	Tilapia Picatta
DAY 46	Apple Torte	Pepperoni Pizza	Gnocchi with Tomato & Wine Sauce

DAY 47	Apple Torte	Veggie Coq Au Vin	Turkey Burgers
DAY 48	Deli Meat & Veggie Antipasti	Veggie Tagine	Sausage with Bell Peppers
DAY 49	Yogurt with Caramelized Figs	Zoodles with Mushroom Sauce	Stuffed Leg of Lamb
DAY 50	Squash & Fruit Bake	Halibut Parcel	Seafood Stew
DAY 51	Tuna Croquettes	Garlicky Prawns	Steak with Yogurt Sauce
DAY 52	Chicken Tagine	Pasta with Veggies	Tuna in Wine Sauce
DAY 53	Yogurt Waffles	Beans & Quinoa with Veggies	Turkey Burgers
DAY 54	Cabbage Casserole	Shrimp Casserole	Seafood Bake
DAY 55	Shakshuka	Spinach & Tomato Sandwich	Asparagus Risotto
DAY 56	Avocado & Eggs Toast	Chickpeas Wrap	Stuffed Steak
DAY 57	Potato Gratin	Four Cheese Pasta	Eggplant Lasagna
DAY 58	Ham Quiche	Lentil Falafel Bowls	Pepperoni Pizza
DAY 59	Blueberry Clafoutis	Couscous Stuffed Bell Peppers	Pasta with Shrimp
DAY 60	Mushroom Galette	Toasted Ravioli	Salmon with Capers

	BREAKFAST	**LUNCH**	**DINNER**
DAY 61	Mixed Veggie Muffins	Asparagus Risotto	Couscous with Cauliflower & Dates
DAY 62	Potato Omelet	Four Cheeses Pizza	Chicken Tagine
DAY 63	Cheesy Spinach Bake	Lentil & Quinoa Casserole	Gnocchi with Tomato & Wine Sauce
DAY 64	Avocado & Eggs Toast	Lamb Koftas	Peas & Feta Sandwich
DAY 65	Cabbage Casserole	Salmon with Avocado Sauce	Seafood Bake
DAY 66	Chicken Tagine	Halibut Parcel	Four Cheese Pasta
DAY 67	Deli Meat Antipasti	Eggplant Parmesan	Octopus in Tomato Sauce
DAY 68	Yogurt Waffles	Chicken Wrap	Mussels in Wine Sauce
DAY 69	Mushroom Galette	Pasta with Beef	Veggie Tagine
DAY 70	Shakshuka	Gnocchi with Tomato & Wine Sauce	Rice & Seafood Paella
DAY 71	Chicken Tagine	Lentil Falafel Bowls	Zucchini Pizza
DAY 72	Blueberry Clafoutis	Gnocchi with Tomato & Wine Sauce	Steak with Yogurt Sauce
DAY 73	Yogurt Waffles	Tuna with Olives	Quinoa & Lentil Soup
DAY 74	Squash & Fruit Bake	Greens & Carrot Salad	Lamb Koftas
DAY 75	Stuffed Mushroom	Zoodles with Mushroom Sauce	Pepperoni Pizza
DAY 76	Multi-Grain Bread	Veggie Coq Au Vin	Tuna in Wine Sauce
DAY 77	Potato Gratin	Lentil Falafel Bowls	Turkey Burgers
DAY 78	Summer Squash Gratin	Four Cheese Pasta	Salmon with Capers
DAY 79	Tuna Croquettes	Tuna in Wine Sauce	Gnocchi with Tomato & Wine Sauce
DAY 80	Deli Meat & Veggie Antipasti	Salmon with Avocado Sauce	Mussels in Wine Sauce
DAY 81	Ricotta Pancakes	Garlicky Prawns	Sausage with Bell Peppers
DAY 82	Apple Torte	Tuna Sandwich	Meatballs Soup
DAY 83	Yogurt with Caramelized Figs	Beans & Quinoa with Veggies	Stuffed Leg of Lamb
DAY 84	Mixed Veggie Muffins	Chicken Wraps	Curried Chickpeas & Veggies
DAY 85	Blueberry Clafoutis	Eggplant Parmesan	Tilapia Picatta
DAY 86	Ricotta Pancakes	Salmon with Capers	Tomato Braised Beef
DAY 87	Potato Omelet	Four Cheeses Pizza	Baked Veggie Stew
DAY 88	Mixed Veggie Muffins	Lentil & Quinoa Casserole	Wine-Infused Lamb Shank
DAY 89	Yogurt with Caramelized Figs	Shrimp Casserole	Tilapia Piccata
DAY 90	Avocado & Eggs Toast	Asparagus Risotto	Lamb Koftas

CONCLUSION

The Mediterranean diet has been around since ancient times, although different countries will have different takes on it. It shows the blend of culture and the rich history behind this cuisine. As if to prove that fact, this diet emphasizes fresh, colorful, and varied healthy foods and limits your intake of processed foods. With this cookbook, your plate will never look boring again.

One reason why the Mediterranean diet is so popular has to do with its realistic approach to dieting. You are not removing any food groups from your diet. The most you will do is limit how often you will have certain kinds of food, giving you a better chance of sticking to the diet.

You will not be counting calories or macronutrients or restricting your eating to a certain time. That means the diet is very easy to follow.

This diet also has many proven benefits. For one, it helps improve your heart health, brain health, and aids in weight loss. All of this is possible because the diet incorporates a lot of healthy foods.

But eating is only one piece of the puzzle. Many Mediterranean people also have a lifestyle that helps keep them fit and healthy. It also helps if you give their lifestyle a go or try to follow some healthy habits.

The Mediterranean people lead a colorful, high-energy, and active lifestyle. So, the first thing you want to do is to get active. In addition to working out, of which you only need 5-15 minutes every other day, you should go out more often. That means walking to places if they are not that far away. You get to enjoy the outdoors and get some cardio in while you are at it.

This lifestyle also emphasizes your social life as well. That does not mean you need to make many friends. Rather, you want to deepen your relationships with the people you truly care about.

There are many ways to do this, but considering that you have a massive list of delicious Mediterranean dishes to choose from in this cookbook, why not invite them for dinner once in a while and introduce them to this style of cuisine? Sharing stories and laughter over a meal is one of the quickest ways to bond.

The best time to start this diet is right now. After that, it is up to you whether you go all in with the philosophies of the Mediterranean diet or take things slow. Although, it must be said that the sooner you follow this diet, the better your health will be in the long run. The best thing about this diet is that you can still enjoy all your favorite foods, and with the help of this cookbook, you might discover new dishes to love.

With that said, take good care of yourself and enjoy this colorful and delectable Mediterranean cuisine!

Printed in Great Britain
by Amazon